OUR PENTECOSTAL BIRTHRIGHT

CHARLES HARRISON MASON

Our Pentecostal Birthright

Copyright© 2007 by Joseph T. Williams

Reprint Copyright© 2019 by Joseph T. Williams

ISBN 10: 1-938373-32-4

ISBN 13: 978-1-938373-32-9

LCCN: 2019948039

Printed in the United States of America

1st Printing October 2007

2nd Printing October 2019

All Scripture quotations are taken from the Holy Bible, King James Version, unless otherwise indicated.

All rights reserved. No part of this publication may be reproduced, stored in a retrieval system, or transmitted in any form or by any means, electronic, mechanical, photocopy, recording, or any other; except for brief quotations in printed reviews, without the written permission of the publisher.

Table of Contents

Introduction 1

Chapter 1 What is the Spirit Saying to the Church? 12

Chapter 2 Our Pentecostal Birthright, the Blessing and
          Identity Theft 17

Chapter 3 Creating the Right Kind of Climate 26

Chapter 4 No More Patches No More Spills 48

Chapter 5 Workers Together with Him 60

Chapter 6 Remember, Consider, Imitate 70

Chapter 7 It's Time to Make a Change 89

Chapter 8 Issues and Answers 99

Chapter 9 The Blessing of Homecoming 114

About the Author 119

ACKNOWLEDGMENTS

First and foremost, I give honor to God, the Father Almighty. I thank him for saving me through his Son's death on the cross, and

for sanctifying, baptizing, and filling me with the Holy Spirit. Lord, thank you for the holy heritage with which you have blessed my family.

I am most grateful to and for Brenda, my wife of 48 years, our four children Joseph DeLawrence, Alston Titus, JoRenda Larnell, and Brenae DeLena, and our eight beautiful grandchildren. As a family we have been richly blessed in being allowed to serve together in ministry. Four generations of our family have been involved in the Church of God in Christ, and with God's continued blessing, that legacy will continue. I thank God for the foundation laid out by my father, Bishop D. Lawrence Williams, my mother, Cora McCollough Williams, and our peculiar treasure, Mother Janette Williams, who married my father and raised his 14 children as though we were her own.

I would also like to thank the Refuge Church of God in Christ family, which has been so supportive of every aspect of our ministry. God bless my siblings, Leroy, Dempsey, Lenora, Jessie,

Evelyn, Robert, Helen, William Dove, Sarah, Gloria, Ruth, Charles Daniel, David, and Samuel. I praise God for my godmother, Mother Annie Bailey, and for the privilege of having Bishop Mason lay hands on me. I praise God for my mentor Bishop Samuel Green, the saints of the Second Ecclesiastical Jurisdiction of Virginia, the Board of Superintendents, my co-laborers, and all the pastors, elders, mothers, missionaries, and friends who have supported the cause of Christ. May God continue to bless the memory of the saints who have gone on and the lives of the saints who still live. Their prayers and words of wisdom and encouragement have brought me to this place in my life.

I gratefully acknowledge the support and encouragement of Higher Standard Publishers. I could not have completed this project without the specific and personal assistance of Mr. and Mrs. William and Selena Owens, CEO and Vice President of HSP, and the gracious editorial assistance of Mr. Seth Styers.

Finally, in the words of Mother Willie Mae Rivers, "All of the glory, the honor, and the praises all day belong to God." And as our Presiding Bishop Charles Blake says, "I see you in the future and you look much better than you do right now." Saints continue to pray for me that I will be all that the Lord has called and created me to be.

Pastor Joseph T. Williams

October 2007

INTRODUCTION

During the centennial celebrations of the Azusa Street Revival and the founding of the Church of God in Christ, I was called upon by the Holy Spirit to reflect on these events as well as the individuals who pioneered them: William Joseph Seymour (1870-1922), the catalyst for the Azusa Street Revival and Charles Harrison Mason (1866-1961), the founder of the Church of God in Christ.

Filled with the Holy Spirit, these anointed men brought the Church back to its origins. While the Pentecostal Church is often associated with the Protestant Reformation, the fact remains that the church rose from the Pentecost long before Martin Luther's 95 Theses. The Pentecostal Church is grounded firmly in the foundations of the original Christian church described in the Book of Acts, which was, as Bishop Melvin Clark once stated, "fervently fundamental, earnestly evangelical, and purely Pentecostal.

God used Bishop Seymour to bring about a Pentecostal revival that would sweep through the nations and change the face of Christianity forever. In addition to bringing forth a renewed emphasis on the baptism and work of the Holy Spirit in the church, Bishop Seymour challenged the social order of

American society. His services were fully integrated and free of gender bias. Color and gender lines were washed away in the blood of Jesus from 1906-1909 at the least. Bishop Seymour wrote in the First Edition of the Apostolic Faith Newspaper, "We are not fighting men or churches, but seeking to displace dead forms and creeds and world fanaticisms while living practical Christianity. 'Love, Faith, Unity' are our watchwords and 'Victory through the atoning blood' our battle cry." This message of equality was as important to Bishop Seymour as was the message of tongues and spiritual gifts, together creating the backbone and emphasis of the Pentecostal doctrine.

Likewise, Bishop Charles Harrison Mason taught and embraced the message of equality. The Church of God in Christ appears to have been the only legally incorporated Pentecostal Church in the early 20th century. As such, ministers bearing his credentials were recognized by civil authorities and were entitled to certain economic advantages, like clergy cards for traveling. As a result, large numbers of whites obtained credentials carrying Bishop Mason's name. According to the Enrichment Journal, between 1909 and 1914 there were as many white Church of God in Christ ministers as there were black ministers, and all carried Bishop Mason's credentials and incorporation.

Bishop Mason wasn't completely trusted by all, though. The FBI kept a file on Bishop Mason because he was a pacifist, which led them to believe he was anti-government. While he was certainly anti-war, Bishop Mason proved himself pro-America by selling bonds to support our country during war.

Though he associated with white ministers, Bishop Mason preserved and maintained the essence of African American worship traditions, including praying, shouting, dancing, and ecstatic utterances. He preached and taught holiness and sanctification as a way of life, not a religion.

The Enrichment Journal published an article describing the efforts of Bishops Mason and Seymour. A summation:

> "It is clearly significant that Seymour and Mason, two African Americans, were used of God to bring about the most important religious movement of the 20th century. These men wanted to demonstrate spiritual empowerment through unity. The unique interracial and intercultural dynamics of both Azusa and the founding of the Church of God in Christ, however, accented both holiness of character and power to witness in an unusual demonstration of love and equality in the body of Christ. In this respect, it powerfully reminds us that the fullness of Pentecostal power will elude those who seek for power in their ministry above that of Christ-like character.
>
> The outpourings of the Spirit at Samaria (Acts 8) and among the Gentiles (Acts 10) taught early

Christians that God's redemptive work transcends racial and cultural lines. Fallen humanity always accords such differences more important than what God designed and by so doing tyrannizes His creative handiwork. Because they had now been "baptized into Christ" and "put on Christ," Paul alerted the Galatian Christians, "There is neither Jew nor Greek, there is neither bond nor free, there is neither male nor female: for ye are all one in Christ Jesus" (Galatians 3:28).

The Azusa Street revival illustrated the fundamental truth about the acquisition of spiritual power: The desire to love others and win the world for Christ begins with brokenness, repentance, and humility."[1]

In summary let me make the following points: First, Seymour and Mason had a desire to break down walls of race, gen- der, and socio-economic class. Second, they were men of prayer. Everything that happened at Azusa and in the founding of our church was grounded in prayer. Third, their character was impeccable, no doubt in part due to their background with the holiness movement. Fourth, they pursued Christ's attitude, even when betrayed. And in their humility, they did not limit the work of God. Lastly, they

---

[1] Copyright '2005 Enrichment Journal The General Council of the Assemblies of God 1445 North Boonville Avenue, Springfield, MO 65802-1894 Frank Bartleman, Azusa Street (South Plainfield, N.J.: Bridge Publishing, 1980)

allowed the Holy Spirit to lead and they did not presume to know more about God than God himself.

While reflecting, I was reminded that I first learned of these great fathers in the Gospel from my own father, Dempsey Lawrence Williams. My father was one of the most remarkable and fruitful men I have ever had the privilege of knowing. His seemingly insignificant beginning gave no indication of the fruitful life he would lead. My father was born into a family of personal piety and devotion. Shortly after the Azusa Street Revival they became members of the Church of God in Christ, and at the age of twelve my father received the baptism of the Holy Spirit. As a young man he had dreams seeing himself preaching in Jerusalem on the day of Pentecost, a privilege God later granted him.

In 1935, Bishop C.H. Mason appointed my father to the Goff Street Church in Norfolk, Virginia. It was the church Bishop Mason had started himself immediately following the Azusa experience in 1907. At the time of my father's appointment, the church had about 60 members. During those early years he was a trailblazing evangelist, planting and establishing churches. Because of my father's faithfulness, God used him to foster and develop the congregation into a thriving church of nearly 2,000 members before he went home in 1971. He became the Bishop of the Second Jurisdiction in 1958, and God used him again to multiply 35 churches into 80 before his death.

My father sowed seeds into the lives of countless people, many of whom have become great leaders, pastors, and bishops. Some of the leaders even served on the General Board of the Church of God in Christ, including Bishop Ithiel Clemmons, Bishop Samuel Green, and Bishop Levi Willis. My father himself served on the first General Board. During the turbulent years following Bishop Mason's death, it was my father, the chair of the Board of Bishops, who steered the church on the right course for its future and maintained unity in the process. He oversaw the writing of the church's current Constitution, which was published after his death.

What elements came together to make my father's life so productive? How did he become a follower of the same caliber of Seymour and Mason?

He was a Man of prayer

My earliest memory is hearing my father walk into my room and throughout the house praying for his family. It was his custom to rise in the early morning hours and walk through the house praying. He would go into each room praying over his children; sometimes I would wake up to hear him. He would be quietly praying with that kind of groan the old saints had. Most of the time he would lay hands on us, and I would lie still and listen as he prayed for us name by name. Then I would fall into a deep sleep, knowing I was loved. My father never visited anyone, sick or well, without praying for them. He would often quote from a hymn by James Montgomery.

Prayer is the soul's sincere desire,

Uttered or unexpressed;

The motion of a hidden fire,

That trembles in the breast.

Prayer is the burden of a sigh,

The falling of a tear;

The upward glancing of an eye,

"When none but God is near.

Prayer is the simplest form of speech

That infant lips can try;

Prayer the sublimest strains that reach

 The Majesty on high.

Prayer is the contrite sinner's voice

Returning from his ways;

"While angels in their songs rejoice,

And cry, "Behold he prays!"

Prayer is the Christian's vital breath,

The Christian's native air;

His watchword at the gates of death;
He enters heaven with prayer.

The saints in prayer appear as one,
In word, and deed, and mind;
While with the Father and the Son
Sweet fellowship they find.

Nor prayer is made on earth alone;
The Holy Spirit pleads:
And Jesus, on the eternal throne,
For sinners intercedes.

O Thou by whom we come to God,
The Life, the Truth, the Way!
The path of prayer thyself hast trod:
Lord! Teach us how to pray.

He was a Student of Scripture

My father spent much time reading and studying and encouraged us to do the same. One of our daily routines was to pray and quote Bible verses before each meal. Sometimes we would read Exodus 20 and Ecclesiastes 3. Other times each of us had to quote specific verses like Ephesians 4: 32 and I Timothy 4: 2. Sometimes he would put money in our Bibles to ensure we at least picked them up and flipped through. My father's life of study led to his being one of the most profound preachers of his day. He traveled the world preaching the Gospel, eventually getting his chance to live out a dream and preach at the World Pentecostal Conference in Jerusalem on the day of Pentecost in 1958.

He Sought True Revival

Our church was a hot bed for revival. Prayer meetings were held twice daily and sometimes early in the morning. We often had all night prayer times and three-day shut ins accompanied by fasting. Most of the evangelists he brought in were praying evangelists.

He preached and lived sanctification and holiness.

He was known in the community as the sanctified preacher. His lifestyle was exemplary, and he lived the life he preached. He was fruitful and productive in society, as well as church.

My father was given good seed, which he planted

in the good ground of his life and the ministry for which he produced: media ministries, magazines like The Voice and The Present Truth, radio, television.

He Believed in Community Outreach

My father believed the church should lead the community in caring for the less fortunate. His community outreach programs included low income housing aid, child daycare, a baby clinic, ministerial associations, and encouraging entrepreneurial enterprises for barbers, beauticians, florists, contractors, realtors, nurses, and educators.

One day while studying I came across this translation of Hebrews 13:7-8: "Remembering those who have led you and have spoken the word of the Lord to you, considering the results of their conduct, imitate their faith. Jesus Christ is the same yesterday, and today, and forever more." Bursting before my eyes was a concept, we should all follow, particularly the words, "considering the results of their conduct imitate their faith." This little treatise will address just that. If we are going to impact our church and our world, we need to remember, consider, and imitate the saints' faith. Our founding fathers changed the landscape of the 20th century. Our challenge is to do the same here and now in the 21st century.

Chapter 1

WHAT IS THE SPIRIT SAYING TO THE CHURCH?

In the last two years (2007=2008) several key national leaders have been called home, including the founder's wife, Mother Elsie Mason; his daughters; General Board Member Wives Mother Wells, Mother Williams, Mother Green, and Mother McKenny; Presiding Bishop G.E. Patterson; General Secretary A.Z. Hall.

Taking note that 2006 was the centennial year of the Azusa Street Revival and 2007 is the centennial year of the founding of the Church of God in Christ, it seems God is trying to tell us something. True, people die every day, but I am made to wonder what the Lord is trying to say when so many of a movement's key people die relatively close to one another. Even in my own church we buried several key members between June and October of 2004, a devastating loss. Among those were our Church Mother, Mother Alston; our Chairman Deacon, Deacon Cleveland O'Neal; an up-and-coming young minister, Minister Chauncey Cooper; Mother

Dozier; and Mother Williams. We began to wonder if we were cursed. Had we done something to offend God? Why were our people being taken home so suddenly?

It was during this season of perplexity in 2004 that God took me to Numbers 33, out of which he began to speak to me. This chapter lists all the places Israel camped during its wilderness wandering. I was trying to figure out why God would have me read this chapter when I came across verse 38, which reads, "And Aaron the priest went up into Mount Hor at the commandment of the Lord, and died there in the fortieth year after the children of Israel were come out of the land of Egypt, in the first day of the fifth month. "

The passage stuck in my spirit, but I still had no clue what it meant. The idea of the "40th year" kept resonating in my mind until I realized the wandering was only to last 40 years. Aaron's death was a sign, a reminder to the Israelites that their wandering was nearly over. Israel needed to prepare to cross over into the Promised Land. As I continued to read in that 33rd chapter, I discovered that the wandering was not quite over. Aaron's death was only an indication that the end was near. When the Israelites reached Jordan in verse 50, God re-instructed them as to what they had to do in order to enter the Promised Land. Numbers 33:50-52 reads,

"And the LORD spake unto Moses in the plains of Moab by Jordan near Jericho, saying, Speak unto the children of Israel, and say unto them, When ye are passed over Jordan into the land of Canaan; Then ye shall drive out all the inhabitants of the land from before you, and destroy all their pictures, and destroy all their molten images, and quite pluck down all their high places. "

At that time God spoke to me, saying I was about to move into the next season of my ministry. I felt his voice saying, "You are about to move, not into the next level, but into a new and different place. You are about to move into your place of destiny and purpose. I am letting you know ahead of time so that when you get to that place you will be ready."

Then the Lord reminded me of some family history. Between 1949 and 1951, I lost my biological mother, my grandmother, and my uncle. In December of 1951, my father married Janie Flood Williams, and by 1952, several of my older siblings were married. Along with other young adults in our church, my brothers and sisters began to have children, first natural and then spiritual. In retrospect, it is clear that this change was an indication of what was going to happen spiritually. My father's ministry began to grow rapidly. The Goff Street Church, which had around 100 members in 1950, grew to over 1,000 members by 1960. God worked in my father and brought about great change in his ministerial life. He became a bishop in Virginia after having been a state overseer.

Additionally, he became our church's representative to the World Pentecostal Conference, President of the Hampton University Minister's Conference, Chairman of the Board of Bishops, the main resource person for the Church of God in Christ manual of 1971, and one of the original General

Board members. My father began to fulfill his purpose and destiny and did so until his death in 1971. Dempsey Lawrence Williams left a legacy that included the construction of two church buildings, the organization of the COGIC Hospital/Insurance Fund, the development of Williams Village in Virginia Beach, and the signing of the documents that finalized the construction of the COGIC Memorial Homes for the Elderly in Norfolk Virginia, the first of its kind in the state. With my mother's death, could my father have known all this would take place? Did my father have any idea of the depth, breadth, height, and length his ministry would take on after my mother died? What could have felt like the end was actually the beginning.

With that in mind, is it not significant that so many influential people in our movement died in the 100th year of our church's history? Or that the founder's wife passed during the Azusa Centennial? We must be ready to embark on the next step of this journey. We must be prepared to fulfill our purpose and destiny. Is the church hearing what the Spirit is saying? This era in our church's history is ending. God is allowing the old guard to die so he can bring a new era of leadership.

The first step in our journey toward new leadership is a mourning period for the deaths of our loved ones. I believe we tend to keep going as if nothing has happened. We seem to mourn as we go, if at all. In biblical times people took 30 days to mourn, as in Numbers 20:29, "And when all the congregation saw that Aaron was dead, they mourned for Aaron 30 days, even all the house of Israel." And when I speak of mourning, I mean more than draping a chair or having a moment of silence during the first few services after someone has passed. Mourning is a time of weeping, reflection, and sorrow. It is a time of anxiety over the future. Unfortunately, political advancement and pressure to move forward leave us with little time to mourn. Would the world come to a grinding halt if we actually stopped to mourn? I believe it is our duty to take time as a church to reflect and cry. Only then can we heal and move forward.

So many of our key people have gone home during the last few years, yet we as a church were often unaware of their passing. We must stop and reflect on what God is saying and doing. If we will, God will reveal that he is pre- paring us to move to a higher place of praise.

Chapter 2

OUR PENTECOSTAL BIRTHRIGHT. THE BLESSING AND IDENTITY THEFT

Genesis is full of stories about sibling rivalry Cain and Abel, Ishmael and Isaac, etc. The story of Esau and Jacob, the twin sons of Isaac and Rebekah, is also a familiar one. It was prophesied that the brothers were two nations in one womb, but it was also said that they would be separated and the older would serve the younger. This would have seemed strange because in Jewish tradition the firstborn son had certain privileges and responsibilities.

The Old Testament teaches that the first fruits of everything belong to God. The first represents the rest of a group, and through the blessing of the first the rest is also blessed. The firstborn became the priest of the family, had a double portion of inheritance allotted him, and inherited the judicial authority of his father, as we see in 2 Chronicles 21:3, "And their father gave them great gifts of silver, and of gold, and of precious things, with fenced cities in Judah: but the kingdom gave he to Jehoram; because he was the firstborn."

The Church of God in Christ is the first fruit of Pentecostalism and the first church to be born out of the Azusa Street Revival. Do we have an understanding of what that means? Do we realize who we are and what we have? The birthright and the blessing belong to us. We are called to be the spiritual leaders of this Pentecostal movement. The judicial authority and the double portion inheritance are ours. In the days of our founding fathers we understood this role and walked in it as well. People came to us for verification and validation. We issued the credentials. In a sense we defined what it meant to be Pentecostal. Our numbers alone point to the fact that we have a double portion. The world talks of megachurches and of single churches reaching out to several places, but we are one church in 10,000 locations. Our Constitution is read and copied by those who have come behind us, as well as our ordination procedures, our worship style, and our doctrine. Much like Joseph, the Church of God in Christ wears a coat of many colors that signifies our blessing and high favor with the Lord.

The Church of God in Christ is the first born of the Azusa outpouring, but have we sold our birthright for a bowl of porridge? Have we chosen to feed our bellies for instant gratification and popularity? Esau gave up his birthright and lost his blessing to his brother who deceitfully smelled like him, felt like him, and tried to sound like him. Many people in the world today try to look like us, sound like us, and act like us. Are we willing to lose our birthright to these people, to embrace those who seek to replace us? Why do we long for this bowl of porridge? We are starving for our own gain rather than longing for God to be glorified.

As important as the birthright is, it cannot stand alone. The birthright must be accompanied by the blessing because the blessing is what enables us to carry out the authority, purpose, and destiny of the birthright. God first blessed Adam in the Garden of Eden. When God created Adam, he spoke purpose and meaning into his soul, saying, "Be fruitful, and multiply, and replenish the earth ,and subdue it: and have dominion over the fish of the sea, and over the fowl of the air, and over every living thing that moveth upon the earth" (Genesis 1:26-28). From that time on, the sons of God have spoken blessing into and over their children's lives. Abraham blessed Isaac; Isaac blessed Jacob; Jacob blessed his twelve sons.

I find Hebrews 11:20-21 to be quite a challenge to my thought life. This chapter is known as the "Heroes Hall of Faith" because it lists men who accomplished great things for God. And while the exploits of Isaac and Jacob are not listed, these men are included in the chapter because they blessed their sons and grandsons. This passage exhibits the importance of biblical blessing in the Christian faith, as it is written, "by faith Isaac blessed Jacob and Esau concerning things to come. By faith Jacob, when he was dying, blessed both the sons of Joseph; and worshipped, leaning upon the top of his staff."

In the case of Esau, Jacob not only stole the birthright, he stole the blessing. The blessing that was to be given the firstborn now belonged to the younger. It looked as though all hope was lost, but when we read Genesis 36:6-8, we see differently:

> "And Esau took his wives, and his sons, and his daughters, and all the persons of his house, and his cattle, and all his beasts, and all his substance, which he had got in the land of Canaan; and went into the country from the face of his brother Jacob. For their riches were more than that they might dwell together; and the land wherein they were strangers could not bear them because of their cattle. Thus, dwelt Esau in mount Seir: Esau is Edom. "

Here, when Esau realized he had lost it all, he cried to his father for another blessing. And when Isaac blessed Esau, he blessed him so that he had as much as Jacob. The brothers had so much that they could not live together. The land would have been stripped bare and the rivers and brooks would have dried up, so they had to be separated as was prophesied from the beginning when it was written in Genesis 25:2 3, "And the LORD said unto her,

> *Two nations are in thy womb, and two manner of people shall be separated from thy bowels; and the one people shall be stronger than the other people; and the elder shall serve the younger."*

We must learn that being separate and distinct is not necessarily a bad thing.

When we have given up our eternal birthright for a temporary pleasure, there is still hope for us in God. Even if the blessing has been stolen, we have recourse. We need to cry out to our Father and ask his blessing because our lives depend on it.

In this seventh year of the 21st century, in this double jubilee year of our church's history, when everything that has been held back is to be released, in this year of prosperity God says, "I will restore to you the years that the cankerworm, the palmerworm, the locust, and the caterpillar have eaten." He will return our birthright. He will give us another blessing and the glory of the latter house will be greater than that of the former house. Our Father says, "You may have been sold into slavery like Joseph, but you will soon awaken in the palace. The enemy may have come and taken your wives and children and all your possessions like David, but you need only cry to me, encourage yourselves in me, then go and recover it all."

Keep in mind that Jesus Christ is the firstborn of God. Because we are saved in Christ, we too are firstborn heirs to the Kingdom. We are seated in heavenly places in Christ Jesus and God has blessed us in him, so we must take it back. We must take it all back.

Even if we have failed and lost our birthright because of our own foolishness, we must understand God's love is for people. We must maintain our confidence in God and his promises. God told Bishop Mason that there would never be a place large enough to hold his flock if he took the name, he gave him and preached holiness. Names in the Bible had great significance because they revealed something of the character of the person so named. Our name reveals who we are. It speaks of the nature and character of our being. We are the Church (the anointed assembly) of God (belonging to God as his treasure) in Christ (positioned in his Son).

My own firstborn son, Joseph De Lawrence Williams, once pointed me toward one of the greatest biblical stories concerning firstborns. It was between God's firstborn Israel and Egypt's firstborn children. In Egypt, the firstborn of Pharaoh ruled. Each dynasty was led by the firstborn of the firstborn of the firstborn, so it was a firstborn of Pharaoh who enslaved God's firstborn nation, Israel. When God was ready for his people to be free, he had Moses tell Pharaoh to let Israel go. Pharaoh refused and God responded by destroying the firstborn of Egypt. In Exodus 12:29 we read, "God honors the firstborn and will judge those who do not value that relationship. "

We must be sure that we do not dishonor our birthright or take it for granted. My son also says Esau was the first victim of "Identity Theft." If we, the Church of God in Christ, are not careful we will find ourselves in a similar situation. Our disrespect for our own birthright allows others to receive the blessing that belongs to us.

I am reminded of a song we once sang regularly at the end of our communion services.

> Hold on O Church of God
>
> Hold on O Church of God
>
> Hold on O Church, hold on O Church
>
> Hold on O Church of God

Other verses would ensue as we shook hands and embraced one another.

> Hold on in Jesus' name
>
> Hold on in one accord
>
> Hold on until he comes

Yes, God has given us a place in history, but he has given us a place in the here and now, as well as the future. We need to occupy our place until he comes. Having done all to stand, we're giving up no ground.

> We're giving up no ground,
>
> We got a cause we're fighting for.
>
> Devil we're not gonna take no more!
>
> No ground, we're giving up no ground.

We're absolutely, positively glory bound.

We're not giving up no ground.

Can you feel the lateness of the hour?

Can you feel the battle going on?

Don't give up when you stumble.

Soldiers lose their way.

Just tune your ear to always hear.

When the trumpet sounds.

We're giving up no ground.

I said we're absolutely, positively glory bound.

We're giving up no ground!

Chapter 3

CREATING THE RIGHT KIND OF CLIMATE

As I meditated on the lives of Bishop Mason, Bishop Seymour, and my own father, I could hear the Holy Spirit clearly say to me, "If you want their kind of results, imitate their faith. If you want their kind of fruitfulness, maintain their kind of climate. You can't just create an atmosphere; you must create and maintain a climate. Imitate their faith and you will have the same results because I am the same yesterday, today, and forever."

Every now and then the Holy Spirit will take me on a scriptural search. First, he took me to Joshua 1:5, which reads, "There shall not any man be able to stand before thee all the days of thy life: as I was with Moses, so I will be with thee: I will not fail thee, or forsake thee. " Then the Spirit took me to the burning bush in Exodus 3:2, which reads, "And the angel of the Lord appeared unto him in a flame of fire out of the midst of a bush: and he looked, and, behold, the bush burned with fire, and the bush was not consumed." Next, God took me to Joshua 5:14-15, saying,

"And he said, Nay; but as captain of the host of the Lord am, I now come. And Joshua fell on his face to the earth, and did worship, and said to him, What saith my Lord to his servant? And the captain of the Lord's host said unto Joshua, loose thy shoe from off thy foot; for the place whereon thou standest is holy. And Joshua did so."

Of course, by now my curiosity had peaked. I asked God what he wanted me to see and understand. The Holy Spirit then responded, "Consider their results and imitate their faith, but don't expect the same manifestations." God was with Moses in the burning bush, and he was with Joshua as the captain of the Lord's host. Different manifestations, but the same God yesterday, today, and forever.

Moses' role was that of a deliverer. He was called to lead Israel out of Egypt, through the wilderness, and to the Promised Land. His was a ministry of guidance and direction, thus God's manifestation to Moses was a pillar of fire, which provided light, warmth, and direction. And for forty years Moses led and directed. Joshua's role was that of a warrior. He was to take Israel into the Promised Land, which was already occupied. He had to fight every step of the way for the next forty years. Thus, God's manifestation to Joshua was the captain of the Lord's host. The same God was with both men. The Lord, however, manifested himself in different ways because each had different responsibilities.

What God has purposed us to do in the 21st century is quite different than what our founders did in the previous century. I don't think anybody is using potatoes and other roots to preach, as Bishop Mason did back in the day; he was dealing with an agricultural society. Most of our ministry today takes place in urban centers, so our purposes, callings, and challenges are different. However, the God of Charles Harrison Mason is also the God of Charles E. Blake. Their callings and ministries are different, and the Holy Spirit will manifest himself differently according to each ministry's need, but the Lord is always faithful and remains the same yesterday, today, and forever.

As I see it, one of our problems is that we are stuck in yesteryear. We long for the good old days. Yet how often does God tell us in his Word to try something new? The events at the turn of the 20th century was new to the church. But at the time, the Holiness churches fought the Pentecostal experience. Many of them died out because they would not accept the change God was placing in their lives. God wants to do a new thing in our beloved Church of God in Christ. Are our ears open to listen and our hearts open to receive? His manifestation to us and in us will be according to our purpose and destiny. The fruit I am to produce will be manifested differently in my life and ministry than in my father's, so I should not expect it to be the same. Through this truth, I should know that Jesus will be the same yesterday, today, and forever.

Be Fruitful and Multiply

The first thing God said to man after creation was, "Be fruitful and multiply." Scripture tells us that God's plan and purpose for the church include both natural and spiritual fruitfulness. Throughout the New Testament we are admonished to be fruitful. This is clearly seen in John 15:1-16:

> *I am the true vine, and my father is the husbandman.*
>
> *Every branch in me that beareth not fruit he taketh away: and every branch that beareth fruit, he purgeth it, that it may bring forth more fruit.*
>
> *Now ye are clean through the word which I have spoken unto you.*
>
> *Abide in me, and I in you. As the branch cannot bear fruit of itself, except it abideth in the vine; no more can ye, except ye abide in me.*
>
> *I am the vine, ye are the branches: He that abideth in me, and I in him, the same bringeth forth much fruit: for without me ye can do nothing.*
>
> *If a man abideth not in me, he is cast forth as a branch, and is withered; and men gather them, and cast them into the fire, and they are burned.*
>
> *If ye abide in me, and my words in you, ye shall ask what you will, and it shall be done unto you.*

Herein is my Father glorified that ye bear much fruit; so, shall ye be my disciples.

As the Father hath loved me, so have I loved you: continue ye in my love.

If ye keep my commandments, ye shall abide in my love; even as I have kept my Father's commandments and abide in his love.

These things have I spoken unto you, that my joy might remain in you, and that your joy might be filled.

This is my commandment, that ye love one another, as I have loved you.

Greater love hath no man than this, that a man lay down his life for his friends.

Ye are my friends, if ye do whatsoever I command you.

Henceforth I call you not servants, for the servant knoweth not what his lord doeth: but I have called you friends; for all things that I have heard of my Father I have made known to you.

Ye have not chosen me, but I have chosen you, that ye should go and bring forth fruit, and that your fruit should remain that whatsoever ye ask the Father in my name, he may give it you."

This, among other passages, raised several questions for me:

What kind of fruit are we producing?

What do we need to produce fruit?

What kind of climate must we create to produce fruit?

What Kind of Fruit are we Producing?

Statistical analysis published February 20, 2006 by the George Barna Research Group in Ventura, California shows us that there is often little difference between Christians and Non-Christians. The concept of holiness is woven throughout the Bible and is one of the foundational teachings of many Protestant churches. From Old Testament passages like Leviticus 19:2 - "Be holy because I am holy"- to several dozen New Testament passages where God's people are described as holy, there is little doubt that holiness is a central tenet of the Christian faith. However, this nationwide survey conducted by The Barna Group indicates that most adults remain confused, if not daunted, by the concept of holiness.

Holiness is Possible

Overall, nearly three out of every four adults (73%) believe it is possible for someone to become holy, regardless of their past. Only half of the adult population (50%), however, says they know someone they consider to be holy.

And that's more than twice as many who consider themselves to be holy (21%).

The views of born-again Christians are not much different from the national averages. Among born-again adults, three-quarters (76%) say it is possible for a person to become holy, regardless of their past. Slightly more than half of the born-again Christians (55%) say they know someone they would describe as holy. And roughly three out of ten born-again Christian (29%) say they are holy, which is marginally more than the national norm.

The adults most likely to say they know someone they consider to be holy are those who describe holiness primarily as possessing a positive attitude toward God and life. Adults who think of holiness as a spiritual condition, on the other hand, are among the least likely to identify anyone they know as holy.

The Meaning of Holiness

When pressed to describe what it means to be holy, adults gave a wide range of answers. The most common reply was "I don't know," offered by one out of every five adults (21%). Other popular responses fell into categories such as "being Christ-like" (19%), making faith your top priority in life (18%), living a pure or sinless lifestyle (12%), and having a good attitude about people and life (10%). Some less common responses included focusing completely on God (9%), being guided by the Holy Spirit (9%), being born again (8%), reflecting the character of God (7%), exhibiting a moral lifestyle (5%), and accepting and practicing biblical truth (5%). Once again, the responses of born-again and non-born-again adults were virtually identical. Holiness is a matter embraced by the church, but it is not one that many Americans adopt as a focal point of their faith development. This is partially because barely one-third of Americans (35%) contend that "God expects you to become holy." A larger share of the born-again public believes God has called them to holiness (46%), but that portion remains a minority of the born-again population.

Evangelicals, revolutionaries, people with a biblical worldview, and ethnic born-again adults are the types of people most likely to say that God expects them to become holy. In each of these segments, a majority stated they firmly believe God expects them to be holy. The survey results also indicated that young adults (age 39 or younger) are less likely than middle-aged and older adults to believe that God expects holiness of his people.

Christians Have Same Incidence of Divorce

Although many Christian churches attempt to dissuade congregants from getting a divorce, research confirms a finding identified by The Barna Group a decade ago (and further confirmed through tracking studies conducted each year since): born-again Christians have the same likelihood of divorce as do non-Christians.

Among married born-again Christians, 35% have experienced a divorce. That figure is identical to the outcome among married adults who are not born-again: 35%. The Barna Group noted one reason the divorce statistic among non-born-again adults is not higher: a larger proportion of that group cohabits, effectively side- stepping marriage - and divorce - altogether. The study states, "Among born-again adults, 80% have been married, compared to just 69% among the non-born-again segment. If the non-born-again population were to marry at the same rate as the born-again group, it is likely that their divorce statistic would be roughly 38%, marginally higher than that among the born-again group, but still surprisingly similar in magnitude."

Barna also noted that it analyzed data regarding the ages at which survey respondents were divorced and the ages at which those who were Christian accepted Jesus Christ as their savior. "The data suggest that relatively few divorced Christians experienced their divorce before accepting Christ as their savior," the group explained. "If we eliminate those who became Christians after their divorce, the divorce figure among born-again adults drops to 34%, statistically identical to the figure among non-Christians." The researcher also indicated that a surprising number of Christians experienced divorces both before and after their conversion.

Multiple divorces are also unexpectedly common among born-again Christians. The Barna Group's figures show that nearly one-quarter of the married born-again population (23%) gets divorced at least twice.

Consequently, the survey exhibited that divorce varied somewhat by a person's denominational affiliation. Catholics were substantially less likely than Protestants to get divorced (25% versus 39%, respectively) Among the largest Protestant groups, those most likely to get divorced were Pentecostals, while Presbyterians were the least likely.

Contradictions Regarding Religious Beliefs

More than four out of five Americans claim to be Christians. Nine out of ten adults own a Bible and most adults read the Bible during the year. A great majority claims it knows all the teachings of the Bible. Given that how can so many people say Satan does not exist. That the Holy Spirit is merely a symbol, that eternal peace with God can be earned by good works, that truth can only be understood through the lens of reason and experience? How can a plurality of our citizens contend that Jesus committed sins, or that the Bible, Koran and Book of Mormon all teach the same truth?

In a sound bite society, you get sound bite theology, Barna lamented. Americans are more likely to buy into simple sayings than a system of truth that takes time to and concentration to grasp. People are more prone to embrace diversity, tolerance and feeling good than judgement, discernment, righteousness and limitation. People are more focused on temporal security than eternal security and its temporal implications. Hopefully once Christian leaders comprehend this, we can be more devoted to effectively challenging the superficial spirituality of our nation. As Paul wrote in the letter to the Galatians, we are only fooling ourselves; God will not be mocked."

Some population segments are notorious for avoiding church. For instance, 47% of political liberals are unchurched - more than twice the percentage found among political conservatives (19%). African Americans are less likely to be unchurched (25%) than whites (32%) or Hispanics (34 %). Asians, however, double the national average: 63% were unchurched! Single adults continued a historic pattern of being more likely than married adults to stay away from religious services (37% versus 29%, respectively).

The statistics don't lie. Several other beliefs have infiltrated the minds of Americans and are causing further harm to the truth of Christ:

- Compared to 63% of all adults, 86% of born-again Christians believe "the Bible is totally accurate in all of its teachings."
- 77% of born-again Christians believe they "personally have a responsibility to tell other people their religious beliefs" compared to 51% of all adults.
- Nearly all born-again Christians (98%) say their religious faith is very important in their life, as opposed to 52% of all adults.
- Nearly half of born-again Christians (46%) agree that Satan is "not a living being but is a symbol of evil." About one-third of the born-again population (33%) believes that if people

can earn a place in Heaven if they are good enough.

- 28% of born-again Christians agree that "while he lived on earth, Jesus committed sins, like other people," compared to 42% of all adults.

- Born-again Christians are more likely than non-born-again individuals to accept moral absolutes. Specifically, 32% of the born-again population says it believes in moral absolutes, compared to just half as many (15%) non-born-again people.

In many communities the church is irrelevant. It is creating little impact, if any. Instead, the world is impacting the church. One of the most astounding truths I have come across is that God never called us to be Christians. We were called Christians first at Antioch by the unbelieving world. God called us to be saints (Romans 1:7 and I Corinthians 1:2).

Spiritual Climate that Produces Fruit

After leaving the Azusa Revival, the late Bishop Mason came to Norfolk, Virginia to take in the manmade wonders of the Jamestown Exposition, but one early morning during his prayer time, the Holy Spirit forbade him to go. Bishop Mason turned to the Lord, asking why he had been led to Norfolk. After much travail of soul, he surrendered to God and began a revival meeting on the street at the Norfolk and Portsmouth Ferry Terminal.

He chose to speak on Luke 13:3-5, *"Except ye repent ye shall likewise perish."* Hearts and doors were opened simultaneously. A hall was secured, and services continued day and night. After the saloon keepers had the hall shut down due to a loss of business, Bishop Mason and a few believers secured another meeting place. The group was persecuted there to the extent that they had to move once again. It was then the Holy Spirit's fire finally fell.

The Azusa Revival was a direct result of much prayer. Few great things are accomplished outside of deep and fervent prayer. The great day of Pentecost was the direct result of the disciples' continuing prayer and supplication with the women, with Mary the mother of Jesus, and with his brethren. Prayer is an essential aspect in developing a productive climate of growth.

We know what the Bible says about good seed and good ground, but what does it say about climate? Scripture does not specifically mention the word climate, but the concept is described many times. One of my favorite passages comes from Joel 2:12-19. The verses reach a pinnacle in 18-19 when God promises fruit.

This passage informs us that fruit must have good ground to grow and develop. They must have the right climate. While pondering this idea. I did a modest study on pineapples, and this is what I found. The pineapple is a tropical or near tropical climate (except in greenhouses) to low elevations between 30°N and 25°S. A temperature range of 65°- 95° (18.33 ° - 45° C) is most favorable, though the plant can tolerate cool nights for short periods. Prolonged cold retards growth, delays maturity, and causes the fruit to be more acidic.

First natural, then spiritual. We can't gown any kind of fruit in any "kind of climate. Certain fruit require warm climates. They require more than warm spring and cool summers. Notice that pineapples can tolerate cold weather for a while but prolonged cold weather retards growth, delays maturity and causes fruit to become more acidic. What a concept for the church. We are trying to grow saint in a cold climate, and it isn't working.

There is a tremendous difference between building an audience and growing a church. When we go to sporting events, it does not matter who's in the stands because we are only watching the players- the group of spectators watching the players. But the church must never be a group of spectators, watching participants.

Our churches may have great crowds, but we must produce saints. An indispensable ingredient for producing saints is the climate in which they are raised. Like pineapples, saints need a hot climate. While we can tolerate cold temperatures for a season, we cannot thrive, and our fruit becomes more acidic. We become self-righteous, judgmental, immature, self-centered, and critical. Instead of searching God's will, we are crying for formulaic Christianity—"Three easy steps to prosperity", "Four things you must do to receive blessings", "How to live a happy life", etc. As Christians, we are privileged to seek the face of God, to know him intimately. But instead, we come to church to get our fix, our spiritual high, and go back home to finish going through the motions of stagnant Christian life. Looking again to the second chapter of Joel, we are given instructions on how to develop a climate for growth:

- Turn to the Lord with fasting, weeping, and mourning.
- Sanctify a fast.
- Call a solemn assembly.
- Sanctify the congregation.
- Weep between the porch and altar.

And what is God's response? He will send us corn, wine, and oil. When we work good seed into good ground and develop the right climate, God sends the produce.

The Bible also speaks of fruitful fasting in Isaiah 58:9-11. God promised to make us like a well-watered garden when we fast according to his word. A climate is developed through obedience to the Lord. But how can we know what the Lord wants us to do if we don't spend time with him in prayer? I don't understand why churches don't schedule regular prayer meetings. I was teaching in our AIM Convention several years ago, and I spoke on some of our church's history. Imagine my shock when licensed missionaries came up to me afterwards and explained to me that they had never been in a tarry service. And we wonder why we have so many lukewarm Christians in our churches. When was the last time we declared a national call to prayer for our church? We have gone through some tremendous times without a call to prayer and fasting. While our national days of fasting are Tuesday and Friday, are we all participating, or are we content to walk in stagnation?

With regard to our spiritual journey, Christians are called to look toward our Lord for wisdom and life lessons for living righteously. Jesus never made a move or decision without extended times of prayer. At the beginning of his ministry he spent 40 days in prayer and fasting. He spent the night in prayer before choosing the twelve disciples and before his Crucifixion. The early church followed his pattern of prayer at its beginning in Acts. It prayed over choosing the original deacons and over sending Paul and Barnabas on their first missionary journey.

Bishop Mason never made decisions without prayer. When he appointed my father pastor of the Mother Church in Virginia, he spent much time in prayer. At the time, a divide appeared in the church over who would supervise the entire state, as well as the local church to which my father was assigned. Through prayer, Bishop Mason made that decision and avoided dissension. He was able to unify the church rather than divide it, and in doing so, helped to strengthen the body of Christ.

We often have difficulty hearing God's voice in our hearts. Although Jesus said his sheep know his voice, it can be hard to hear him because of our carnal desires. Spending extended time in prayer and fasting helps us get past our flesh and into the Spirit to hear from God's voice.

The Prayer of Desperation

Prayer often manifests itself in different forms, and at times it is the prayer of desperation that emerges in our hearts. Hannah was barren until she cried out to God in her soul's desperation. By yielding the fruit of her womb to the Lord, Hannah glorified him and put trust in his will. In her desire to be fruitful, Hannah prayed deeply from her heart and touched God's throne.

According to I Samuel 1:11, Hannah prayed,

> *"O Lord of hosts, if thou wilt indeed look on the affliction of thine handmaid and remember me, and not forget Your maidservant, but will give Your maidservant a son, then I will give him to the Lord all the days of his life, and a razor shall never come on his head."*

Note that Hannah's spiritual leader had no understanding of her story. Here's was the woman who would bring forth a son who would anoint the first two kings of Israel. She was about to give birth to the man who would usher in a new day for God's people. But Eli, the priest, was in the dark.

Now suppose this story was an allegory with Hannah representing the church and Eli representing our Leadership. What a pitiful situation. While the church seeks to set the tone and direction needed to bring renewal in the coming years, our leaders have no clue as to what is going on.

The answer to Hannah's prayer had earth-shaking consequences that carried beyond her family and Israel. Samuel's life and ministry affected the world in both his time and ours. Similarly, God wants the saints of the Church to reach our respective local bodies, our nation and the world. We need to pray and fast in desperation for a new kind of leadership that will usher in a new form of government and authority, in the church and in the world.

When God needed someone to lead Israel through the wilderness, he chose Moses who followed the Lord's will and helped deliver God's people to the Promised Land. But a different type of leadership was needed when Israel reached the Promised Land. God raised up Joshua to be a warrior leader in a time of battle. He was a man of faith who dared to fight in faith. Leaders are chosen by God for their usefulness in the present moment. The Church of God in Christ does not need another C. H. Mason or another J. O. Patterson. It needs a humble servant who can lead us into the fight for righteousness and holiness. The Church of God in Christ needs a leader who can dispossess the enemy and distribute the land, one who can help us win our inheritance and take the nation for God.

Tarrying: The Blessedness of Waiting on God

I grew up in a tarrying church and we believed that tarrying had many positive benefits even if it wasn't required to receive the baptism of the Holy Spirit. Every Monday night, the saints would gather and sometimes we didn't leave until early Tuesday morning. Even though the service was designed for new believers to receive the baptism in the Holy Spirit, many old timers would come to assist the new converts. However, sometimes the new converts were on their own because the older believers were getting through for themselves. It didn't take me long to learn that tarrying was about more than receiving the Holy Spirit—it was about what happens when we wait on God. The Lord provides us numerous examples of tarrying saints throughout the Bible.

In Exodus 2:4, God instructs Moses to come up into the Mountain and "be there." Verse 16 says that God didn't speak to Moses until the seventh day. Moses had to wait six days without food or water before the Lord spoke to him. What did Moses get out of tarrying in God's presence? He received a plan detailing how the Lord intended to create a habitat in the midst of Israel. God intricately informed Moses on how to properly build the tabernacle, from the size to the supplies.

Daniel set his face to seek the Lord in fasting and prayer for twenty-one days in Daniel 9. And what was his reward? He received an understanding of the course for God's people.

Jesus only instructions to his disciples for receiving the Holy Spirit was to tarry until they were endued with power from on high. What was the result of their obedience? The outpouring of the Holt Spirit which ushered in the church. The power of the Kingdom was released for all who believe.

Unfortunately, because tarrying is not necessary to receive the Holy Spirit, some Christians have disregarded the practice altogether. But God is calling the church back to a place of waiting on Him. This is not a passive waiting, but an active waiting. We are tarrying in His presence until the endowment of power comes. Relatively few people attended the tarry meetings, but the rewards reaped for our church cannot be overstated. These warriors of Christ kept the church hot so the saints could grow, develop, and be fruitful for the Lord. Many still reap the fruit of their labors.

We must understand that the harvest is the result of our faithful actions. We plant. We water. We nurture and we reap. Our actions give glory to God, but our inheritance is based on our salvation in Christ—a sanctification the likes of which we cannot fathom. Eyes have not seen, ears have not heard, neither has it entered into the heart of man the things God has prepared for those who love him. Our inheritance is prepared by God by virtue of the fact that he is our Father. It is not earned, merited, or deserved. As gracious as this gift is, we still have to mature to utilize it effectively. Galatians 4:1 reads, "Now I say, that the heir, as long as he is a child, differeth nothing from a servant, though he be lord of all." Similarly, the Apostle Paul wrote in Corinthians 13:11, "When I was a child, I spake as a child, I understood as a child, I thought as a child: but when I became a man, I put away childish things." Maturation is the process by which God prepares us to handle our inheritance.

Chapter 4

NO MORE PATCHES—NO MORE SPILLS

Are we following Christ's instructions? In Mark 2:21-22, our Lord said,

> *"No man also seweth a piece of new cloth on an old garment: else the new piece that filled it up taketh away from the old, and the rent is made worse. And no man putteth new wine into old bottles: else the new wine doth burst the bottles, and the wine is spilled, and the bottles will be marred: but new wine must be put into new bottles."*

Jesus had been questioned about his disregard for the tradition of fasting. After explaining why his disciples did not fast, he goes into a short discourse about patches and spills.

We cannot continue patching this old garment. With each new patch, we rip away more of the original garment, so why not get a new garment? It's time to move on, to start a new.

Christians have wasted enough of God's new wine trying to keep it in old wineskins that continue to burst and break. The anointing continues to run out, thus accomplishing nothing. God granted this wine to His believers to enjoy, not to waste.

New Wine in New Wineskins

Is God doing a new thing in the Church of God in Christ, and if so, are we open to the new thing God is doing. While the faithful actions of Bishop Mason were brand new at the time, if we are still trying to do what Bishop Mason did, we are living one hundred years in the past. We have utilized his form and organization for one hundred years, and now God wants to get a new wine skin for a new wine of the 21st Century. The new wine is the same kind of anointing and power, even the same doctrine, but with a new package that can breathe and grow.

I know very little about wine, so I did some research. I learned that when new wine is put into the wineskin or bottle, it is untainted, unfermented grape juice. I also learned that grapes are the only fruit that need nothing else added to ferment. In Scripture, new wine refers to substance.

What is our substance? Who are we? We are called to be more than a hand-clapping, foot-stomping, tongue-talking Pentecostal church. Jesus refers to new wineskins as packaging. In America, we love name brands, but in other countries, they prefer to see the food through the packaging; they want to seek the bread rather than the name.

When it comes to the church, the substance needs to be seen through the packaging. Name brand packaging may look nice, but it makes us look like everyone else. Age is our defining feature and leaves us in a sad state. While other churches have followed in our footsteps, have we moved forward and gotten new wineskins"? Are we following the Lord or has our true substance been replaced with contrived forms of worship?

The Pentecostal church is more than speaking in tongues. Everybody has that, and they get it anywhere. We have reduced baptism in the Holy Spirit to tongues, singing and shouting, but God has blessed us with more than tongues. We have reduced it to experience that is often merely repeated over and over. Christians are called to live such a life walking in the Spirit. In fact, we are privileged to live such a life, but we devalue it when we limit the blessings of God. We know all about speaking in tongues and prophesying, but few of us know the excellent way of love. Several passages of Scripture come to mind with regard to these concepts. Luke 4:1-14 reads:

> *And Jesus being full of the Holy Ghost returned from Jordan, and was led by the Spirit into the wilderness, being forty days tempted of the devil. And in those days, he did eat nothing; and when they were ended,*

he afterward hungered. And the devil said unto him, If thou be the Son of God, command this stone that it be made bread. And Jesus answered him, saying, It is written, That man shall not live bread alone, but every word of God. And the devil, taking him up into an high mountain, shewed unto him all the kingdoms of the world in a moment of time.

And the devil said unto him, All this power will I give thee, and the glory of them: for that is delivered unto me; and to whomsoever I will I give it. If thou therefore wilt worship me, all shall be thine. And Jesus answered and said unto him, Get thee behind me, Satan: for it is written, Thou shalt worship the Lord thy God, and him only shalt thou serve. And he brought him to Jerusalem, and set him on a pinnacle of the temple, and said unto him, If thou be the Son of God, cast thyself down from hence: For it is written, He shall give his angels charge over thee, to keep thee: And in their hands they shall bear thee up, lest at any time thou dash thy foot against a stone.

And Jesus answering said unto him, It is said, Thou shalt not tempt the Lord thy God. And when the devil had ended all the temptation, he departed from him for a season. And Jesus returned in the power of the Spirit into Galilee: and there went out a fame of him through all the region round about.

Notice in verse one Christ is *"full of the Holy Ghost,"* but in verse 4 he comes in the *"power of the Spirit."* What happens to Jesus in the passage to cause this change? By verse 14 he has been tried and tested, and the Holy Spirit has manifested himself in power.

Acts 1:8 reads,

"But ye shall receive power, after that the Holy Ghost is come upon you: and ye shall be witnesses unto me both in Jerusalem, and in all Judaea, and in Samaria, and unto the uttermost part of the earth."

We don't receive power until we have the Holy Spirit; even still, I believe many people have the Holy Spirit, but he does not have them. They speak in tongues but do not function in the power of the Spirit. These people are not hypocrites. They are genuinely saved. Though they love the Lord, these people haven't the faintest idea of what it means to walk in the Spirit.

Accordingly, Galatians 3:3 reads, *"Are ye so foolish? Having begun in the Spirit, are ye now made perfect the flesh?"* Many of us begin in the Spirit but are now trying to be perfected by works of the flesh. Our church began in the Spirit, but many have come to believe that voting and elections are going to perfect us. Do we think that our strategic planning sessions and our back-room politics are going to help this church become what God intended it to be?

In Philippians 3:3, the apostle Paul writes, *"For we are the* circumcision, *which worship God* in *the spirit, and rejoice* in *Christ Jesus, and have no confidence in the flesh."*

Paul breaks down several aspects of the Christian life in this passage. We are the circumcision (we are saved and sanctified); we worship God in the Spirit (we kiss toward, bow down before, lose ourselves in the presence of the Lord); we rejoice in Jesus (Pentecostals know plenty about this singing, shouting, dancing, and running around the church). Paul finishes the verse with a concept that many or most of us struggle with. We are to have no confidence in the flesh. A life focused on carnal pleasures leads to death. Our lives are supposed to be focused on Christ through the Spirit. Being baptized in the Spirit is not enough; we must learn to walk in him as well. God has given us the new wine of the Holy Spirit, but we cannot use it to get drunk in the Spirit.

Paul expands upon this point in Ephesians 5:18, *"And be not drunk with wine, wherein is excess; but be filled with the Spirit."* Notice the verse does not say to be drunk with the Spirit, rather it says be filled with the Spirit. I can think of no passage in the Bible that teaches spiritual drunkenness. To be filled with the Spirit is not to be out of control but to be controlled or led. Pastor John McArthur, who is neither charismatic nor Pentecostal, offers an incredible illustration of what it means to be filled with the Spirit. While many Christians use the idea of a glass filled with water, Pastor McArthur illustrates the indwelling of the Spirit with a hand-filled glove. The glove can do nothing in and of itself; it can only be effective when it is filled with and guided by the hand.

The glove can hammer a nail, drive a car, and even pick up a dime when it is filled with the hand. Likewise, when we are filled with the Spirit, we don't fulfill the lust of the flesh, but are instead guided by the Spirit. God wants our church to be Spirit-filled and Spirit-led. He wants us to operate in the power of the Spirit. The old hymn "Stand Up for Jesus" has a line that says, "The arm of flesh will fail you; you dare not trust your own." We began as a Spirit-led church. Are we now being perfected by the wisdom of men or the wisdom of God?

A biblical concept that somehow escapes us is that of the mind of Christ. We have put so much emphasis on being filled with the Spirit that we have overlooked what the Bible says about the mind of Christ. Maybe God was trying to tell us something by speaking of it throughout the Bible:

- Isaiah 55:8 - *For my thoughts are not your thoughts, neither are your ways my ways, saith the Lord.*
- Romans 7:23 - *But I see another law in my members, warring against the law of my mind, and bringing me into captivity to the law of sin which is in my members.*
- Romans 8:7 - *Because the carnal mind is enmity against God: for it is not subject to the law of God, neither indeed can be.*
- Romans 8:27 - *And he that searcheth the hearts knoweth what is the mind of the Spirit, because he*

maketh intercession for the saints according to the will of God.

- Romans 12:2 - *And be not conformed to this world: but be ye transformed by the renewing of your mind, that ye may prove what is that good, and acceptable, and perfect, will of God.*

- Romans 15:6 - *That ye may with one mind and one mouth glorify God, even the Father of our Lord Jesus Christ.*

- I Corinthians 1:10 - *Now I beseech you, brethren, the name of our Lord Jesus Christ, that ye all speak the same thing, and that there be no divisions among you; but that ye be perfectly joined together in the same mind and in the same judgment.*

- I Corinthians 2:16 - *For who hath known the mind of the Lord, that he might instruct him? But we have the mind of Christ.*

- Ephesians 4:23 - *And be renewed in the spirit of your mind.*

- Philippians 1:27 - *Only let your conversation be as it becometh the gospel of Christ: that whether I come and see you, or else be absent, I may hear of your affairs, that ye stand fast in one spirit, with one mind striving together for the faith of the gospel;*

- Philippians 2:2- *Fulfill ye my joy, that ye be likeminded, having the same love, being of one accord, of one mind.*

- Colossians 3:12 - *Put on therefore, as the elect of God, holy and beloved, bowels of mercies, kindness, humbleness of mind, meekness, longsuffering;*

- I Timothy 1:7 - *For God hath not given us the spirit of fear; but of power, and of love, and of a sound mind.*

- Philemon 1:14 - *But without thy mind would I do nothing; that thy benefit should not be as it were of necessity, but willingly.*

- Hebrews 8:10 - *For this is the covenant that I will make with the house of Israel after those d(9s, saith the Lord; I will put laws into their mind, and write them in their hearts: and I will be to them a God, and they shall be to me a people.*

- 1 Peter 4:1 - *Forasmuch then as Christ hath suffered for us in the flesh, arm yourselves likewise with the same mind: for he that hath suffered in the flesh hath ceased from sin;*

The mind of Christ is one of humility, service, and sacrifice. His thoughts are revealed to us by the Spirit. *As* the church, we are to have Christ's mind and his voice. The division and strife among us does not come from the mind of Christ. We are not to fight flesh and blood. A key passage regarding spiritual warfare is 2 Corinthians 10:4-5,

> *"For the weapons of our warfare are not carnal, but mighty through God to the pulling down of strong*

holds; Casting down imaginations, and every high thing that exalteth itself against the knowledge of God and bringing into captivity every thought to the obedience of Christ."

I wonder if we can quote this passage, though, with understanding. Everything we deal with in those verses has to do with the mind, imagination, knowledge, thoughts. We strike against demons with full force, but like the demoniac in Luke 8, we need to be, as some old saints would say, clothed in our right mind. I remember an applicable song from back in the day. We sang:

My mind, my mind, my mind is gone.

That old evil mind I had, my mind is gone,

That old sinful mind I had, my mind is gone,

Jesus gave me a brand-new mind; my mind is gone.

New mindsets are gained through intimacy with God, not human effort or reasoning. Having begun in the Spirit are you now perfected in the flesh? To be truly filled with the Spirit is to have the mind of Christ.

I must digress to tell a story of embarrassment. I attended Nyack Missionary College in Nyack, New York, and one Sunday night I took some white, conservative college students to one of our storefront churches. The only Church of God in Christ in the area, the congregation stood fifteen members strong. It seemed as if every person played some type of instrument - tambourines, scrub board, wood blocks, maracas, organ, and piano. Even the pastor played a trombone.

During the testimony service, the congregation began singing the aforementioned song behind Sister Treadwell's lead. I remember her height and lankiness as she moved to the music. Her necklace swung from side to the side and she seemed to become the song. The instruments continued as she sang. Then, a few lines into the song, one brother – a giant of a man - started dancing in the Spirit. Essentially, he was hopping across the floor like a bunny rabbit. At that point the saints really went at it. I don't know if you can imagine the incredulous looks on the faces of my white, evangelical friends. That should have been enough exposure for one night, but in the middle of everything the pastor stopped playing his trombone and blew a whistle. Everything stopped and the saints immediately went back to their seats. The pastor taught that the Spirit of the prophet was subject to the prophet, so when he blew the whistle the Spirit would come under submission. Just as abruptly as everything started, it ended. I was so sure my friends were convinced that our minds were really gone that I wanted to walk back to the dorm alone. I explained all the way home, thinking all the while, "My God, why hast thou forsaken me?"

Chapter 5

WORKERS TOGETHER WITH HIM

As I have grown in the Lord, I have found out that it is harder to come out of the wilderness than to come out of Egypt. Crossing the Red Sea was a matter of following Moses' lead through dry land. The wonders of God were overtly present in the parting of the sea and the deliverance from slavery. God acted alone. But when it came to crossing Jordan, Israel was troubled. With the river at its flood stage, the priests had to step in carrying the Ark of the Covenant with the Jordan overflowing its banks. Then they had to stand there until all the people had passed over and set up memorial stones in the middle of the river bed.

The idea that God has everything in his hands has caused me much personal distress. I remember when God sent our church word that he had given us the city. We shouted and danced and shouted some more. Every Sunday we came together and rejoiced because God had given us the city- good times abounded. But even as we kept shouting, we never got the city. So, I went back to the Word to find out where we missed it. We had only read through Joshua 7:2 before we began shouting. Unfortunately, we failed to read further and find out that God gave specific instructions as to how the Israelites were to take the city. While God gave Israel the instructions, they had to accept and use them. Our church missed that part. We must pay attention to every part of God's Word because taken in pieces or out of context, it cannot impart all its wisdom on our lives. This is how we get messed up. We have to read with understanding and not preconceived ideas. In following God's instructions, we fulfill our duty in working with him.

We have been taught that the Promised Land flows with milk and honey, but we are rarely taught that it is already occupied with enemies stronger and greater than we are. Why is the Promised Land a land of war, one that we must take from an enemy? This truth regarding giants in the Promised Land never occurred to me before. I have read the book of Joshua many times, but this revelatory power hit me between the eyes when I finally opened them. I thought that the Promised Land was just flowing milk and honey. When God opens our eyes, he wants us to perceive and understand a great spiritual truth, so with this new insight I re-read Joshua. With open eyes, I finally realized that the first five chapters are preparation, and the next six chapters are war stories - battle after battle after battle. A new message of God's Word was revealed to me. After forty years of wilderness ty wandering, the Israelites spent the next forty years fighting battles to dispossess their enemies and take the Promised Land. The words jumped from the page, directly at me. How could I have been so blind? Through all the fighting I even began to feel sorry for Caleb and Joshua. Here were two men who had the right spirit, being constantly faithful to God, but they had to suffer with God's disobedient and faithless people for forty years in a wilderness. They were then called to go into the Promised Land to fight for another forty years. I learned that our disobedience and doubt affect not only ourselves, but also those associated with us including family, friends, our congregation, and even the nation.

Another lesson I learned was that God deals with us corporately as well as individually. While we tend to think about ourselves, God is often dealing with an aggregate "us." Do I seriously think that God sends a prophetic word, one that is ministered across the country, just for the sake of me? As a whole, the human race is a self-absorbed people. When the Israelites came out of Egypt, they all came out - every tribe and even a mixed multitude came. When they came to the Red Sea, they all crossed, not just Moses and his family. At Mount Sinai the Law was given to all the people. The manna, the quail, the water out of the rock, they were for all the people.

When Israel rebelled against God and failed to enter the Promised Land, Joshua and Caleb did not get in despite the fact that they believed God. They had to wander with everyone else. When God opens the doors for the church to enter the Promised Land it will not be for a few select individuals. When the saints go marching in, I will be in that number. We will even be caught up together in the Rapture. So why do we think it's all about us? Our human selfishness takes advantage of the love of God. I sometimes come to convince myself that God only loves me as much as he does. This perversion of God's great gift not only devalues it but prohibits God from blessing us further.

Wars are not solo fights. Even though a soldier may be working individually he is still a part of the larger, more complex battalion. Even in Bible times a man rarely fought a battle by himself. When David fought Goliath, he did so as a representative of the armies of Israel. His defeat of Goliath led to the defeat of the Philistines for God's people. His exception is notable only because of his fervent faith in the power and will of God. But for the most part, we are banded together to help one another and to give strength and encouragement. As I have heard said many times, there are no Lone Rangers in God's army.

Lessons on Unity

The Bible has a great deal to say about unity. The saints are called to be unified in Christ; in fact, Christ is supposed to be the only factor that truly unifies us. Through unity we are further blessed by God. Psalm 67:3 reads, *"Let the people praise thee, 0 God. Let all the people praise thee."* Then shall the earth yield her increase. When the people of God honor him like he should be honored, the earth is blessed abundantly. Psalm 133 talks about the blessedness of unity and closes in verse three with, *"…for there the Lord commanded his blessing, even life for evermore."* The blessing is commanded where unity abides.

The apostle Paul writes in Ephesians that we are fitly joined together and compacted by that which every joint supplies. The body of Christ is supplied strength through its joints, its connectedness.

Connectedness in Christ can be easy to do and easy to spot when carried out through the Holy Spirit. For some time, we had worshipped at the COGIC High Rise Home for the Elderly. This ministry itself came about through connectedness. Deacon Armstrong, who was a member of Triumph Church of God in Christ, suggested that I ask Mr. Lemuel Williams if we could use their auditorium on Sundays. An old friend, a member of Faith Temple Church of God in Christ, and the manager of the High Rise, Mr. Williams allowed us to do so. Not only were we blessed with a larger place to meet, but several of the senior citizens who could not get out to church began attending our services. In this instance we were strengthened by that which the joints supplied.

We learned about a week before Christmas, which happened to be on a Sunday that year that the auditorium was going to be used by the residents for their own Christmas service and dinner. We had no place to worship on Christmas, but connectedness helped see us through. One sister started making calls and helped us secure a location. In talking with some members of the local Church of God, we figured they would have an early service and we could use it later in the day, or vice versa. To our surprise we were told they had their service on Christmas Eve and that the building would be available on Christmas Sunday. Overjoyed, we were ecstatic with the news because connectedness in the body of Christ had led to God's blessing our Christmas. We went in on that cold, snowy Sunday morning and the praise and worship was truly of the Lord. God healed Sister O'Neal in her seat, without a prayer line. I said to the Lord, "If this is the place you have for us then let us raise $1,000 this morning." At the time we were doing well to get $500 weekly. I knew that only God could do this for us. As both the Minister of Music and Head Pastor, I sat at the piano making an appeal for a special Christmas offering without saying what I wanted to raise. Unbeknownst to me, my wife's parents, Deacon Fork and Mother Larnell Alston, had already planned to give $1,000 that Sunday morning. The answer to our need for a place to worship and my prayer for a fertile offering was supplied by the joints in the body.

As a congregation, we were trying to purchase new buildings for our church and ministry and had given everything we could. We sold chicken dinners, candy, and a little of everything in between. Now some ministers say that we are not supposed to sell chicken dinners to support the ministry, but I have often wondered why the same ministers believe it is okay to sell books and tapes to support the ministry instead. Is there something ungodly about the chicken? The Lord uses talents of all kinds, from cooks to writers, to support his people. We can all be useful to God's purpose if we are only willing to let him use us. But I digress. We had come down to the day before closing on our new building, but we were $1,500 short. It was Bible study night, and the attendance was not at its usual Sunday Morning numbers. Every factor seemed to be against our new building, for we had scraped the bottom of the barrel and come up empty. After Bible Study I told the saints what we needed. I had no idea how we were going to raise the money that night, but I had that assurance in my soul. While I was addressing the need I saw a member named Paul Hawkins look at his wife Lovie. He walked up to the offering table and presented me with a check for $1,000. He and his wife had already agreed to give it that night. That blessing then inspired the rest of us to find the final $500. Though the times seemed lean and hard with little left for us to do, God used unity to work a miracle and fill our empty pockets.

In being called the body of Christ, we set ourselves up for an excellent illustration of how God causes our physical bodies to work in unity and how this applies to our lives. I Corinthians 12:2-17 reads:

> *For as the body is one, and hath marry members, and all the members of that one body, being many, are one body: so also, is Christ. For one Spirit are we all baptized into one body, whether we be Jews or Gentiles, whether we be bond or free; and have been all made to drink into one Spirit. For the body is not one member, but many; If the foot says, Because I am not the hand, I am not of the body: is it therefore not of the body? And if the ear shall say, Because I am not the eye, I am not of the body; is it therefore not of the body? If the whole body were an eye, where were*

the hearing? If the whole were hearing, where were the smelling?

As the body of Christ, we are dependent on one another for the sake of acting as a unit. Whether interpersonal, interdepartmental, or ministerial, the church relies on relationships within the body to function. And as the leaders of the Church of God in Christ, we are required not only to provide connections to help unify the body, but to help keep these connections connected through an understanding of Christ-like unity.

How can pastors' best encourage unity? By supplying spiritual nourishment, building the body of believers, and knitting the community together with the bonds of peace and love. Ephesians 4:2-3 instructs us:

> *"with all lowliness and meekness, with longsuffering, forbearing one another in love; Endeavouring to keep the unity of the Spirit in the bond of peace."*

In order for the church to function as the Body of Christ, peace and love must reign, the unity of the Spirit is maintained through the bond of peace, not denominational loyalty. Every member of the body of Christ must maintain and fulfill his or her role for the body to work efficiently for the glory of God. Every person is given certain talents and abilities, and when a person becomes saved by the grace of God, these abilities become spiritual gifts to be used according to God's will. As a unified body, we must respect, encourage and develop these gifts.

Additionally, we need to teach and preach and exercise the priesthood of all believers. Church members need to know about spiritual gifts and know that they are able to use them for God. The body of Christ must understand that with these gifts we can operate as a whole rather than a collection of parts. Sometimes we act as a valley of dry bones rather than a cohesive unit. If we submit ourselves to the will of the Lord and commit our talents to his greater good, the Church of God in Christ can enter the 21st century with renewed life and a mission to honor God in all.

Chapter 6

REMEMBER, CONSIDER, IMITATE

This first 100 years has been grand and glorious. The Church of God in Christ has grown from an obscure beginning to one of the largest Pentecostal churches in the world. God has done some awesome things with us and through us. Bishop Mason started with fewer than twenty-five people in the first organizational meeting, and now we estimate a worldwide membership of 6,000,000 or more.

As we prepare for the future we need to reflect on our past. Hebrews 13:7-8 reads,

> *"Remember them which have the rule over you, who have spoken unto you the word of God: whose faith follow, considering the end of their conversation. Jesus Christ, the same yesterday, and today, and forever."*

While verse eight is very familiar, verse seven is often overlooked. Three words break this passage down to its core: Remember. Consider. Imitate. Remember those who led you. Consider the results of their conduct. Imitate their faith.

Remember: Historical Accounts of Each Leader's Ministry

The church is built upon the foundation of the apostles and prophets, and the most important corner stone, Jesus Christ. Our apostle Bishop Mason laid a spiritual foundation that had far reaching effects on the life of the church and nation. He brought about what my cousin, the late Bishop Ithiel Clemmons, called a New Spirituality. Baptism in the Holy Spirit, the operation of spiritual gifts, the renewed emphasis on holiness and sanctification, racial and gender equality, a life of prayer - these concepts formed the bedrock of Bishop Mason's life and ministry. As a leader, his administrative ability was truly remarkable. Instead of trying to do it all, he organized work in manageable pieces that gave others the opportunity to use their gifts and talents. He structured the church so that pastors could make a decent living, and he recognized the need for women's work, departments, and auxiliaries. We are yet building on that foundation today.

Bishop O. T. Jones was the last of the original bishops appointed by Bishop Mason. He developed the Young Peoples Willing Workers (YPWW), which was the training ground for our young people, and he helped to codify our doctrine and teachings.

Bishop J. O. Patterson came into leadership with an ecclesiastical structure that gave us respectability as a church. I am old enough to remember when we were considered a cult. We eliminated the last cult-like visage—the perception of "one charismatic leader." In 1968, we elected our first General Board, and while we had boards before, this was the first to be elected by the General Assembly of the church. This act helped our church become more democratic—one that was led by people rather than a person. Under his leadership we formed the C.H. Mason Theological Seminary to raise a trained and educated clergy. Properties were secured to expand our headquarters, and thus expanded our ministry's base. UNAC, All Saints University, the COCIG Hospital Fund, and the Chaplaincy Ministry were all developed in his twenty-one years of service.

Bishop L. H. Ford was arguably the most colorful of all our Presiding Bishops. While his term in office was short, he did much to restore the recognition of Bishop Mason's legacy and heritage. Bishop Ford restored the Saints Academy and reached out into the political realm, bringing our church more political recognition. While some people question the wisdom of political involvement, we do well to remember what Scripture has to say. God's priests laid hands on and anointed the kings of Israel. Kings once turned to the prophets to discern what God was saying at any given time. Our church leaders need to have the king's ear. Our ministry should not only affect the church, but the nation and world as well, and we can't do that without getting involved.

Bishop C. D. Owens brought the economic perspective into focus. While many of our leaders were prosperous, our church consistently operated in the red, often borrowing money to survive between meetings. But under Bishop Owens, we began putting money aside, buying property, and developing land deals with the city of Memphis. Unfortunately, we wronged Bishop Owens by failing to allow him to finish his term.

Bishop G.E. Patterson was able to bring all those differing perspectives into one. He renewed an emphasis on our history, singing the old songs, Morning Manna, political involvement, and economic stability and accountability. These tributaries all flowed into one mighty stream, thereby strengthening the church. He will probably be regarded as the best preacher among the Presiding Bishops, and history still has more to say regarding his administration.

Our founding fathers were people who operated in the gifts of the Spirit. The 1960s were turbulent years for our church. Our founder died, but the church had to roll on. Like Moses his death was an indication of a new day with new leadership. In our anxiousness to go forth we made some mistakes. When Moses died the Israelites knew that Joshua was to be his successor. I think it was clear to us that Bishop O.T. Jones was to succeed Bishop Mason, but there were a couple of important Scriptural principles that we did not understand at that time. Thank God for progressive revelation.

God told Joshua, *"As I was with Moses, so shall I be with thee"* (Joshua 1:5). However, when we read the story, we discover that the manifestations were different. God appeared to Moses in the burning bush (Exodus 3:2), but he appeared to Joshua as the captain of the host of the Lord (Joshua 5:14). Some of us expected God to be with the new leader in the same way he was with the old, but their purposes were not the same. God used Moses and Bishop Mason to deliver us, to be outstretched arms of faith. The pillar of fire guided, directed, and protected us. The Lord used Joshua differently to bring Israel into the Promised Land.

In order to lead Israel into the Promised Land, God utilized a warrior in Joshua. Israel crossed the Jordan on the "obedient feet" of the spiritual leaders who stood in the water to get Israel across. If we are to enter our place of destiny and purpose, it will be on the obedient feet of our spiritual leaders. Succeeding leaders tried to lead as Bishop Mason did, but we failed to be aware that Bishop Mason's style of leadership changed over the years. He was preparing the way for a new wave of leadership by delegating much of his administrative responsibilities to others. These new delegates were his appointees, those who were to carry the Church of God in Christ onward.

When we took over after Bishop Mason's death, we tried to carry the same administration with a new leader. Unfortunately, our plans didn't work. Bishop Jones actually had his own cabinet that was advising him. The political infighting was fierce and deadly, but it brought us to the place we needed to be. In 1968, almost 40 years ago, we elected our first General Board.

Much of our history has been more like the wilderness wandering, rather than entering the Promised Land. As hard as it may seem to understand, we can get comfortable in the wilderness. If God supplies manna, water, and quail, and keeps our clothes and shoes from wearing out, it becomes easy to develop a welfare mentality. But no matter how wonderful the blessings are in the wilderness; they do not take the place of purpose and destiny for God's people. God has a place for the Church of God in Christ that is far greater than anything we can imagine.

After wandering forty years Israel could have been lazy and unproductive. It had subsisted off the goodness of God and fought a few battles. While Israel had become a warrior nation, it was only under the guidance of God for the sake of entering the Promised Land. God says in Exodus 13:17 that he purposely led them the roundabout way so they would not get discouraged when they saw war. They had to fight hopelessness, laziness, and discouragement. Before letting the devil sell us a bad bill of goods, Christians must see the situation from God's perspective. Have we wandered for the last few years and grown lazy and unproductive? We are now entering the Promised Land; we have to get off of those lazy, unproductive, unfulfilled bones and fight hopelessness and despair. Remember, there are enemies stronger and greater than we are inside the Promised Land, and they will destroy us without the strength and grace of the Lord.

Caleb and Joshua were the only adults to leave Egypt that entered the Promised Land because they had a spirit of faith and obedience. Remember it was the obedient feet of the spiritual leaders that determined their success. I believe that for the Church of God in Christ to be successful in the 21st century, the obedient feet of our spiritual leaders will be essential. We the people have to learn to follow leadership even when we don't see that it's going to be any different. Then we must set up a memorial in the Jordan to remind and inform our children of who God is and what he can do.

When Saul became king of Israel it was because the people wanted a king like the other nations (Samuel 8:5). God was preparing to take them there with David, but in their haste to be like others they got Saul. It was forty years later that God raised up David as king. I can't help but wonder if we followed the same path. We had a lot of meetings and sent letters back and forth across the country. When Samuel was faced with this dilemma, he sought God in prayer. For the Church of God in Christ, though, there does not seem to be much prayer in the records. In biblical times, God, through David, was ushering in a godly line that was to bring forth the Messiah. But the people got ahead of Him. In our efforts to be more acceptable, we have chosen voting over prayer. Each new level of ministry should be preceded by extended times of prayer and fasting. We didn't like the way Bishop Jones led so we went to court, sued, and voted. Now we vote every two years for something or someone, whether we need to or not. What has happened to phrases like, *"It seemed good to the Holy Spirit and us"*?

We now spend more on election campaigns than we did on our entire church budget in the 1968. Oddly enough we encourage our members to pray, but what about our leaders? When do they come together for extended times of prayer?

I am reminded of a story I heard some time ago. In the old days two school-aged church boys had been warned by their principal that if they were late for school they would be suspended. Nearing school, the next morning, they heard the first bell ring. One boy said suggested they stop and pray. The other said, "No, let's run and pray!"

We are taught holiness in worship and conduct. All of us it seems could quote Hebrews 12:14 by heart, but that is only one passage. Holiness and sanctification are biblically present from Genesis to Revelations. I can almost hear my father's voice now, preaching and teaching from these Scriptures.

- Obadiah 17 - *But upon Mount Zion shall be deliverance, and there shall be holiness; and the house of Jacob shall possess their possessions.*
- Luke 1:71-75 - *That we should be saved from our enemies, and from the hand of all that hate us; To perform the mercy promised to our fathers, and to remember his holy covenant; The oath which he sware to our father Abraham, That he would grant unto us, that we being delivered out of the hand of our enemies might serve him without fear, In holiness and righteousness before him, all the days of our life.*

Once we are delivered out of the hands of the enemy, we are to serve God without fear in holiness. There is no fear in Holiness. Jesus came as the horn of salvation to deliver us from fear so we could serve God in holiness. Holiness is not being scared of Hell or God's wrath. Holiness aims at service of the Lord based in Scripture. It seeks to serve God, but in entirely a different sphere than that which most of us understand. This is what Zachariah, father of John the Baptist, alluded to in Luke 1:74. According to Luke, Zachariah and Elizabeth were *"both righteous before God, walking in all the commandments and ordinances of the Lord blameless" (Luke l: 6)*.Scriptural passages have endless wisdom about holiness to speak to us:

- Philippians 2:14-16 - *Do all things without murmurings and disputings: That ye maybe blameless and harmless, the sons of God, without rebuke, in the midst of a crooked and perverse nation, among whom ye shine as lights in the world; Holding forth the word of life.*
- I Peter 1:15 - *But as he which hath called you is holy, so be ye holy in all manner of conversation.*
- I Peter 3:11 - *Seeing then that all these things shall be dissolved, what manner of persons ought ye to be in all holy conversation and godliness.*

In the highest sense, holiness belongs to God (Isaiah 6:3; Revelation 15:4) and to Christians consecrated to God's service, in so far as they are conformed in all things to the will of God (Romans 6:19, 22; Ephesians 1:4; Titus 1:8; I Peter I: I 5). Personal holiness is a work of gradual development. It is carried on under many hindrances, hence the frequent admonitions to watchfulness, prayer, and perseverance. Holiness is not church activities, which are brought to the front, but rather the personal life. It is good behavior, righteous conduct, godly conversation, even tempers, and most importantly, the glorification of God—all aspects primarily belonging to the personal life. The first great aim of the Christian life is holiness of heart and mind. In glorifying God, the most effective way to succeed is by living a holy life. For this very purpose the Christian consecrates himself to God. He gives himself entirely to God. Many New Testament writers refer to this as conversation.

Conversation is generally defined as the goings on of social intercourse (Ephesians 2:3; 4:22), the deportment or course of life. This word is not used in Scripture in the sense of verbal communication from one to another (Psalms 50:23; Hebrews 13:5). In Philippians 1:27 and 3:20, a different Greek word is used. It means one's relations to a community as a citizen, or citizenship.

He whom the Son sets free is free indeed, but there are limits and boundaries. Galatians 5:1 reads,

"Stand fast therefore in the liberty wherewith Christ hath made us free and be not entangled again with the yoke of bondage."

Galatians 5:13 continues,

"For brethren, ye have been called unto liberty; only use not liberty for an occasion to the flesh, but love serve one another."

So, serving God without fear in holiness means I am free to live my life any way I choose as long as it glorifies God and expresses love for others.

Think about being licensed to drive. The state of Virginia assigns a license that allows people to operate a motor vehicle. However, you cannot drive at night without your headlights on. You cannot speed down the road at 95 miles per hour. You must drive a functioning vehicle. There are principles of safety and common sense that must be applied to the driving privilege. Citizens who drive with common sense and safety don't have to be scared of punishment from the police. Similarly, the Christian life, when acted out in reverence for the Lord, is one free of fear of punishment.

Holiness and freedom go hand-in-hand with principles that regulate our activities. What is the difference between a drunken Christian and a drunken sinner? Or the unsaved drug addict and the Christian who uses illegal drugs? Nothing. There is no difference unless the Christian applies principles of holiness to his conversation/manner of life. God wants much more from us than a life of sin; he wants us to serve him in Holiness without fear for the rest of our days. God chose us to be holy before the foundation of the world was established. What does living without fear in holiness mean? This concept is described in Titus 2: 11, *"For the grace of God that bringeth salvation hath appeared to all men."* We are all saved by grace, but that is not the end of the story. The book of Titus continues by saying, Grace instructs us that denying ungodliness and worldly lust, we should live soberly, righteously, and Christ-like in this present world, looking for that blessed hope that is the return of Jesus Christ.

Many people call themselves Christian but aren't holy; they don't serve God. Jesus came to do more than keep people from Hell. He came as the horn of salvation to deliver us from our enemies, and one of our greatest enemies is the idea that we can please the flesh. When we please the flesh rather than God, we are unholy.

What about those who are struggling with habits whatever they may be? First, these people shouldn't be leaders in the church. Members may do so, but we must call the leaders of the church to live above reproach. There is no walking the line when it comes to the examples we set for other Christians. We must understand that there is a difference between struggling and just doing what you want to do. Let me make it absolutely clear that a person cannot serve as a leader in this church in either case. Those who struggle must keep practicing the spiritual disciplines- fast, pray, deny the flesh, attend church, and read and study the Bible. Sanctification is a lifelong process, not a single event. Those who are doing whatever they want to do need to practice the same disciplines with the understanding that life is not about what we want; it is about God and what he wants. It is about serving God and loving our fellow man. Life is a conversation with the Lord and our brothers and sisters. My life should exhibit who I have become in Christ. Life is about my conversation being understood.

I can preach all day on holiness, but in the end, God has already said it better than I ever will. His desire for our holiness is not only for our own good but helps us to glorify him to our greatest extent.

- 2 Corinthians 7:1 - *Having therefore these promises, dearly beloved, let us cleanse ourselves from all filthiness of the flesh and spirit, perfecting holiness in the fear of God.*

- Ephesians 1:1-4 - *Paul, an apostle of Jesus Christ the will of God, to the saints which are at Ephesus, and to the faithful in Christ Jesus: Grace be to you, and peace, from God our Father, and from the Lord Jesus Christ. Blessed be the God and Father of our Lord Jesus Christ, who hath blessed us with all spiritual blessings in heavenly places in Christ: According as he hath chosen us in him before the foundation of the world, that we should be holy and without blame before him in love.*

- 1 Peter 1:15-16 - *But as he which hath called you is holy, so be ye holy in all manner of conversation; Because it is written, be ye holy; for I am holy.*

God had given us great commands to be holy. As followers of Christ, we are called to heed his word and live a life focusing solely on glorifying God with our every action.

I Thessalonians 4:1-8 - Furthermore then we beseech you, brethren, and exhort you the Lord Jesus, that as ye have received of us how ye ought to walk and to please God, so ye would abound more and more. For ye know what commandments we gave you the Lord Jesus. For this is the will of God, even your sanctification, that ye should abstain from fornication: That every one of you should know how to possess his vessel in sanctification and honor; Not in the lust of concupiscence, even as the Gentiles which know not God: That no man go beyond and defraud his brother in any matter: because that the Lord is the avenger of all such, as we also have forewarned you and testified. For God hath not called us unto uncleanness, but unto holiness. He therefore that despiseth, despiseth not man, but God, who hath also given unto us his Holy Spirit.

Consider: Learning from the Examples of Past Leaders

Consider the results of their conduct. What did they produce? How were they fruitful? How did they multiply and replenish? They built the Mason Temple in the 1940s with nickels, dimes, and pennies. The resilience and faith of the early Church of God in Christ was able to take small pieces of anything and mold them into a whole. Small change made buildings and small congregations made millions of followers. We must learn from these examples, considering the results of their faith, and move forward in the 21st century.

Our pioneers have brought forth great and mighty churches and ministries. They produced a great harvest. What are we producing, and how are we producing it? I think somewhere along the way we have forgotten what we are supposed to produce and how we are supposed to produce it. We have the right word and good seed, and we are biblically and doctrinally sound. We have good ground, and our people are some of the best in the world. What else does it take to reap the harvest? Besides good seed and good ground we need the right climate and atmosphere. Just as tropical fruit won't develop in a temperate climate, neither will Christians hot for the Word of God be produced in lukewarm ministry. I think we have settled for producing Christians when God has called us to produce saints. The world called us Christians. God called us saints, and he gave the five-fold ministry the responsibility of perfecting the saints.

In this centennial year of the Church of God in Christ, considering the results of the conduct of Bishop Mason, my father, and the other pioneers of the Church of God in Christ, I wonder what has happened to our church. Bishop Mason was thrown in jail for preaching the Gospel, and while he was praying and praising the Lord from his cell, the judges who sentenced him died. He didn't go around pulling down principalities over towns. When they put him out of town he stayed out until they called him back to pray for rain. When the general church came into Virginia to remove my father all he did was have us talk about his love for God and the church. He didn't bind demons and devils. He stood on his faith.

Imitate: Becoming Leaders in the Mold of Christ

Are we imitating our past leaders' faith, or are we imitating their conduct, behavior, and practices? Are we believing like they believed, and are we getting the same results? Why is it that they were able to do so much with so little? They learned to stand on the principles of God's Word while we remain as the double-minded man who is unstable in his ways. With all we have at our disposal, we should be able to multiply their results exponentially. But first we must have their faith. Our founders stood on their faith and did not compromise with the enemy.

How does that translate into real life? We need less emphasis on tongues and more emphasis on love. It seems that the pulpit wants all the spiritual power but expects the pew to operate in love. We want to exercise power from our positions of leadership, but have the congregations bear the hard times. From the pulpit, we expect our saints to believe, hope, and endure everything we say, but are we leading by example ourselves? Ephesians 5:2 reads, *"And walk in love, as Christ also hath loved us, and hath given himself for us an offering and a sacrifice to God for a Sweet smelling savour."* As leaders of the church, we are called to love as Christ loved and to lead as Christ led. The first step we must take in imitating the faith of our founders and the leadership of Christ is to pray we are hearing and understanding the will of God.

Understanding the Will of God

Matthew 25:26-30 is an eye-opener and, to me, somewhat disturbing passage because it reveals that wickedness encompasses more than societal constructs of what is "bad." The passage reads:

> *"His lord answered and said unto him, Thou wicked and slothful servant, thou knewest that I reap where I sowed not, and gather where I have not strawed: Thou oughtest therefore to have put money to the exchangers, and then at my coming I should have received mine own with usury. Take therefore the talent from him and give it unto him which hath ten talents. For unto everyone that hath shall be given, and he shall have abundance: but from him that hath not shall be taken away even that which he hath. And cast ye the unprofitable servant into outer darkness: there shall be weeping and gnashing of teeth."*

All my life I thought wickedness equaled drugs and promiscuity, but in this parable the Lord calls the servant who produced nothing wicked. God wants more from us than a scared faith that produces little results for fear of taking a risk;

he wants profit for his Kingdom. He wants us to use the gifts he bestowed upon us and bring him a return on his investment. What has the Church of God in Christ done with God's investment? What will we do in the 21st century to bring him profit? By example, as leaders we must understand the will of God so that the Church of God in Christ may honor the Lord through our lives.

Chapter 7

IT'S TIME TO MAKE A CHANGE

Joshua 1:2-3 reads,

"Moses servant is dead; now therefore arise, go over this Jordan, thou, and all this people, unto land which I do give to them, even to the children of Israel. Every place that the sole of your foot shall tread upon, that have I given unto you, as I said unto Moses."

Not only do we need to know the times and seasons, but we need to know what to do. Understand this is a season of change. We love to talk about the past, and that remembrance is important, but we also need to advance without trying to repeat the past. Moses fulfilled his duty and died. He led the people out of Egypt and then through the wilderness for forty years. He taught Israel God's laws and his ways. When Moses brought God's people to Jordan his work was over. And the people mourned his passing and moved forward. It was time for a change and Joshua was prepared to lead. His job was to cross the Jordan and take possession of the Promised Land, and he fulfilled his duty according to the will of God.

We must rearrange our thinking and let go of some of some things to grab hold of others.

- Give up in order to receive.
- Get out of the boat to walk on water.
- Cast your nets on the other side.
- Don't stay in the same place until you die, but cross over the Jordan to the Promised Land.
- Possess the land, and in doing so, take charge of life in the name of Jesus.
- If you want to possess the promises, you must sing over your situation rather than cry.
- Be ready for the blessing.
- Enlarge your tent so that you may grow and develop exponentially.
- Search ad reach deeper, higher, and broader.

We must strengthen our stakes, and build up our foundation, all with the understanding that God is in control. David threw the stone that killed Goliath. But God slew the giant. Moses led Israel out of Egypt, but God parted the Red Sea and caused it to crash in on Israel's enslavers. Joshua fought the battle of Jericho, but it was God who caused the walls to fall down.

We can only overcome our enemy through the blood of the Lamb and the word of our testimony. Christ bas already defeated Satan on the cross, so we can be bold, strong and adventuresome. Take some risks, walk in faith, and enjoy victory because God will protect us. Danger awaits Christianity's saints, but with an understanding, we can live without fear. This is my heritage, and this is how my father built a church, two housing complexes and became an international representative for the church. This is how Bishop Mason built this church on nothing but a promise from God. This is the heritage of all the saints.

Stephen the Martyr was a tremendous deacon. I am sure we all would love to have some Stephens on our board. As tremendous as his work was, he died. But Stephen's testimony in death may have been even more important than his testimony in life. He understood God's will and was unafraid of serving the Lord to the point of death.

After Stephen's death God prepared Philip to spread Christianity from Jerusalem into Samaria. Without the death of Stephen, Philip wouldn't have gone to Samaria to continue the Ministry. Nothing has changed. There is only one prerequisite for revival —death. Once we let the past be the past, we can move forward and bring about great change.

Just as death can be good for the church, sometimes separation is positive as well. When Paul and Barnabas separated, two missionary teams formed out of their departure - one became two. Oh, my church, hear what God is saying to us. The time of mourning over past dispensations is over, and the dawning of a new day has come. This centennial marks a new beginning.

It represents the beginning of a new process for developing wine for the 21st century. It is now time to move, and if we follow the direction of the Lord, we will surely move in the right direction.

- Move from strength to strength: Psalms 84:5-7 is a great passage for today. It reads,

> *"Blessed is the man whose strength is in thee; in whose heart are the ways of them. Who passing through the valley of Baca make it a well; the rain also filleth the pools. They go from strength to strength, every one of them in Zion appeareth before God. "*

- Move from faith to faith: Romans 1:16-17 reads,

> *"For I am not ashamed of the gospel of Christ: for it is the power of God unto salvation to everyone that believeth; to the Jew first, and also to the Greek. For therein is the righteousness of God revealed from faith to faith: as it is written, The just shall live faith."*

- Move from glory to glory: II Corinthians 3:16-18 reads,

"Know ye not that ye are the temple of God, and that the Spirit of God dwelleth in you? If any man defile the temple of God, him shall God destroy; for the temple of God is holy, which temple ye are. Let no man deceive himself If any man among you seemeth to be wise in *this world, let him become a fool, that he may be wise."*

In seeking God's guidance, we must ask when to move and when to stay. The Lord will not try to trick us but will give us signs on when to move. Abraham moved in the time of famine and God blessed him greatly. Isaac sowed in the time of famine and received 100-fold in the same year. Jacob moved in the time of famine because God provided food in Egypt through Joseph. Four lepers sat in the gates of the city and decided to take a chance on going into the enemy's camp. Not only did they find food, but they found enough for themselves and the people in the city.

There is an old country western song that says,

"You got to know when to hold them and when to fold them. You got to know when to go and when to stay, when to run and when to stand."

We must understand that when God says move, he means move.

Some of us know that it's time to move. God has called us to arise and go over our Jordan. We must understand this call doesn't necessarily mean we should leave COGIC and find another church or ministry, but if that is God's call, we should follow. What God is often saying, though, is that we should move from complacency to a place of conviction. We should make things happen ourselves. Instead of criticizing others, we should take charge ourselves. We need to take a chance on God, move out of our comfort zone, and go into the enemy's camp.

Our God makes dreams come true for those who dare. Joseph was a dreamer, but if he'd stayed at home his dreams would have died with him.

God stirs the nest like an eagle. Joseph wasn't going to leave home without a push. He had to be taken to Egypt in order to save his family, so God used his jealous brothers to move Joseph where he was supposed to be. What will God need to do for us to move into place?

The lepers were stirred by their need for food to move from the safety of the city gates into the enemy's camp. How hungry is the Church of God in Christ? What do we want from God and what are we willing to do to get it? Instead of being conformed by our circumstances, we should be transformed by the renewing of our minds. God has called us to arise and cross this Jordan.

Though the river is at flood stage, with the waters dark and rough, we must be willing to put our feet in and show God our faith so he will calm the waters and help us pass. In order to cross the Jordan at flood tide we must possess an overcoming spirit. Fear is not a factor. Timidity is not for the Christ follower. When Israel crossed into the Promised Land, it was willing to trust the Lord at a time of struggle and war.

We must mirror that example and be prepared to trust God as we delve into the 21st century. The Church of God in Christ is called to do so.

Three Applicable Scenarios for the Church of God in Christ

- Scenario One: Having looked at John 9, I believe it is time for us to wash the mud off our eyes, find the right pool, and get fresh vision. We need new strategies and a fresh impartation. If we do so, we will reach the Promised Land.

- Scenario Two: David was away fighting for his life when the enemy came in and took his possessions, his wife, and his children. He and his men cried and wept before the men got upset with him. Then David had to encourage himself in the Lord and seek God's direction.

- Scenario Three: The disciples had followed Jesus for more than three years, experiencing God in new and mighty ways. They put all their hope and confidence in Jesus only to have him crucified. After failing Christ, the disciples became discouraged and disheartened. Having given up and returned to their professions, the disciples encountered Christ after his resurrection. Even though they had been discouraged, they obeyed Jesus' words and caught a great draught of fish.

Then there was the day of Pentecost. All the stories of the Bible led to the crucifixion and resurrection of Christ for the formation of the new church. Because the disciples obeyed the Lord, they experienced the conviction of the Holy Spirit, the salvation of Christ, and the grace of the Father. With God behind them, the Twelve changed the world.

Even when we start fighting and the enemy comes in behind our backs to take the things we love; we have to encourage ourselves in the Lord and seek him for direction. After we have waited and waited for the Holy Spirit and nothing seems to be happening, we must tarry. It is out of obedience that we will eat the good of the land. It is in our obedience that we will receive the blessing of the Lord that maketh rich and addeth no sorrow.

A soldier doesn't march into war without marching orders regarding where to go and how to fight. The same is true for the prayer warrior who must receive prophetic insight to fight effectively on his knees.

Throughout the church there has been a remnant of people being prepared for something significant. It will be a first fruits harvest. During the last year in particular we saw various places where the spiritual climate was being transformed by the injection of God's presence.

When we are able to touch God's heart with our desperation for him, it releases an authority and anointing that literally changes a region. For instance, we were just in a particular city and held a conference that the Lord blessed. Many leaders who were not even a part of the conference called the host pastor and acknowledged that the conference changed the atmosphere over the region. They were seeing a fruitfulness that was not present before the conference. This is an example of how the Lord can change the spiritual climate of a region and impact the entirety of the church. It is a principle of the Kingdom. Throughout the church, the Lord is changing the spiritual atmosphere through churches and regions and establishing boundaries and borders that present the revelation of his kingdom.

Chapter 8

ISSUES AND ANSWERS

We face many issues now and in our future. Our handling of these issues will determine our success as a church in the 21st century.

Financing the Ministry

It seems our leadership is stuck in the past when it comes to financing the ministry. We depend too much on reports and offerings, particularly offerings during meetings and conventions. The Church of God in Christ has too many resources to let this continue. A consistent income will better benefit the church than a sporadic seasonal offering.

We need to develop a tithing system through the churches, each church paying a tithe of their tithes to the national church, and then seeing their contributions benefitting their jurisdiction and the church as a whole.

Many denominations have special days for certain ministries to encourage individuals, businesses, and churches to participate more fully in the church's ministry. Churches and individuals could respond directly to the church's needs rather than through the hierarchy. We should have a national Pentecost Celebration - fifty days of prayer and Bible study related to Pentecost and the Holy Spirit. The package would include study materials, messages, daily devotions, and suggested service materials like scriptures, songs, responsive readings, materials for children and youth, etc. This would serve to bring about unity as well as a stream of revenue for the church. As leaders, we need to call for national days of prayer for our church.

We need to utilize the centennial year to bring attention to the heritage and needs of the Church of God in Christ. Our members could contribute to the centennial celebration, and in doing so raise awareness among members across the country. People would feel as though they had a hand in the everyday goings on of the church and would take pride in our heritage.

Another idea is to create a national media ministry belonging to the entire church rather than certain individuals. Radio, television, print media, they can all be utilized for the glory of God in reaching out to both lost individuals and our own members. Not only would the ministry bring in revenue, it would also add national and international exposure.

A grant-writing office could also be a worthwhile venture, allowing our new ministries to be funded by grants.

The money is there, and the resources are there. We need only take the lead from God and stretch our minds beyond the fund-raising strategies of the past.

We have the resources to do all of this, but some people are more concerned with who gets the credit for the money we receive to build God's Kingdom. We have members who would be honored to serve their church in some of these capacities - doctors, lawyers, educators, engineers, entertainers, and a host of other professions. All our members should be encouraged to strengthen and build our resource pool to help take our church to its place of purpose and destiny.

We also need to be careful stewards of the money we have now. We must focus more on prayer and God's guidance in what to do with the money. The greater good of the church is more important than gaining political power in elections, but if we are going to be political, we need to use the same kind of accountability factors that the government uses when it comes to campaign financing.

Multiple Conventions

We have around eight conferences and conventions every year, and they often become "Hallelujah! Bless Me!" parties. We come to sing and shout and listen to a good word and go home feeling energized. Some of us pick up a few things here and there to help us in our ministry, but most of us just go home having left that knowledge behind. We don't need more of these parties. Oftentimes we elect leaders with vision, and they lose the vision. They get stuck in the rut of doing the same things the same way on the same levels. With our organizational size, leadership skills, and connections our time together could be a lot more productive.

Lack of a National Church-Planting Strategy

We need to perform research to find out where Church of God in Christ churches are needed. Teams need to go into areas and evangelize and plant churches. The Bishop's Council could advise on how to fund each regional church-planting strategy.

Church planters can go to numerous websites and get information on any community in the country, but the Church of God in Christ website could become a one-step informational center. Leaders could visit the site and obtain whatever info was needed for the church- planting process.

We often forget that most of our churches are not mega-churches. Most of them are small, and many are struggling, but they are all loyal to our church. The smaller churches need to feel support from the hierarchy above. Not all of us have the same ability, and not all of us are called to pastor mega-churches.

Instead of discouraging pastors of smaller churches because of their congregations' small sizes, we should encourage them that their work is as important to the Lord as that of the largest church in the Church of God in Christ. With all our national and regional conferences, there is little time left for the local church. The money we spend on travel, hotels, and food would be better spent in giving the people more discretionary funds to support the ministry.

I remember staying in West Memphis during a spring meeting. I could not afford to rent a car or stay in the best hotel, but I was able to catch a ride with another preacher at the same hotel. The meeting lasted only one day, and I had the choice of staying there another day or two or paying more money to get my flight changed. Options for cash-strapped pastors often become limited and expensive.

Multiple conferences and conventions are a thing of the past. We must come together in a new way for a new day. The expression goes, "If it ain't broke, don't fix it," but I wonder if we have just gotten so used to limping that we don't know we are able to walk straight. One well planned and administered "Mega-fest" event would have more far-reaching effects than all of our meetings. We must bring these conferences together and in doing so, we will create unity and make our time together more efficient and cost-effective.

In the early days of our church we had schools in various locations and homes for the sick and elderly. These were supported by local, state, and national entities. We had tremendous building programs all over the country, but these were primarily led by local congregations with occasional help from the national delegation. At this point in our history, though, we aren't doing these things on a national scale. We have General Board members who have connections with the departments of Housing and Urban Development, and Health and Human Services, the Lily, and various other foundations, but the benefits from these connections aren't reaching the ground often enough. Some of those who sit in the General Assembly feel that the members of the General Board have lost touch with what it means to be a struggling pastor. We must relate with pastors, churches, and members from all walks of life. The growth and spread of our denomination requires it.

Quitting Before Submitting

There is a spirit among us, and it is breeding a culture of quitting. We have many with an independent attitude who profile on the national platform but have no affiliation with the church at home. They don't support jurisdictions or districts. We have had some to leave our church because they refused to submit but later come back as leaders. Do we realize what that breeds among everyday members? Followers mirror the attitudes of their leaders, a fact that puts even more pressure on us to lead under the will of God. Those who remain faithful often question their own motives and convictions when they feel their leaders aren't acting in faith. This attitude permeates our church, and while the spirit of independence isn't always a bad thing, we must be more willing to obtain a spirit of interdependence. We must rely on one another so that we may function to our full potential.

Intimidation vs. Impartation

Many leaders since Bishop Mason have led by intimidation. That same anointing flows down from the head to the beard and even the skirts of the garment. Intimidation as a leadership quality seeps into our local delegations and congregations. We even use the fear of God to force people to obey us. Interpretation: "If y'all don't do what I say, God's gonna send you to Hell!" Some leaders have threatened to leave and take resources with them. We don't need leaders cut from this cloth.

When I read about men like Moses, Joshua, David, and even Jesus, I see a different style of leadership. They did not use intimidation. They used impartation. Bishop Mason himself used this style of leadership by appointing bishops and other leaders with whom he had a relationship.

In order to impart we must spend time with others and develop healthy pastoral relationships. We need to share our hearts and our vision, and we need to develop strategies. Our congregations want to be involved; they are seeking people to mentor and develop them to take part in God's good works. Though some may say our church is too large for that now, we must strive to breed relationships grounded in the Word of God and behind the example of Christ.

National leaders need to have the same spirit as our Presiding Bishop, and that establishment will not come through encyclicals, politics, or intimidation. General Board members need to have the same spirit as the Presiding Bishop, and that doesn't happen through the election of twelve men. We need continuity in the Board and a spirit of service, not personal gain. Thank God we have been blessed with a Presiding Bishop who guides and serves the Church of God in Christ in spite of our faults and troubles.

In the early days, men like my father who were selected by Bishop Mason emulated the lifestyle and spirituality of their leader. These days, we often have leaders or potential leaders who are self-serving, prayerless, and greedy. They seem to desire that ignorance and dependence run rampant through their churches. Some twist God's Word for their own benefit. Powerful positioning and acclaim are more important to these false leaders than the Kingdom of God. These are the words of the people.

This responsibility of imparting does not need to be assigned to others; it must be performed by the leader himself. While others can help, a leader must delegate and take on the majority of responsibility himself.

Some perceive General Board members as fathers, while others only see them as older brothers. Leaders will do well to perceive themselves as brothers. We are not going to respond to brothers' the same way we respond to fathers because the relationship is different. Adult children allow fathers certain latitude because of the nature of the relationship, but a spirit of independence can be bred by failing to incorporate members as people of equal spiritual worth. Our members want to be led rather than driven.

The Memphis Miracle

We experienced a great miracle in Memphis a few years ago when white and black Pentecostals came together for the first time since the Azusa Revival and washed one another's feet. And during the convocation of 2006, we experienced an even greater miracle. When Bishop G.E. Patterson embraced Bishop C. D. Owens and recognized him as his only peer, as a Presiding Bishop that is, the Church of God in Christ saw a great example of leadership. We often die with unresolved issues. We act as if we have no problems, even when our lives say otherwise. Leaders often say everyone should live in unity but fail to live out the call themselves. This gesture, though, was one that opened the doors for millions of congregants of the Church of God in Christ to rid themselves of unnecessary, trivial issues.

The miracle in Memphis righted a wrong against Bishop Owens that had festered for years. We put him out of office before his term was up and in doing so, perpetuated an illegal and immoral act. We were wrong and I'm thankful Bishop Owens was embraced and was asked for forgiveness.

Ordination of Women/Women in the Ministry

This has been, and continues to be, a much-discussed issue, and we will continue to talk about it until someone becomes courageous enough to deal with it. We must look at this issue from a biblical perspective, rather than a traditional one. Most of us are unaware that Romans 16:7, Junia is a female name. Paul says she is of note among the apostles. Our teaching that there were no female apostles must change. Junia was one and there must have been some basis for her being so. Women have been permitted to do anything in church men are allowed to do except be ordained. I also fear extreme feminism, but I think we need to line up with the Word in regard to women. We cannot allow our biases to determine this issue. If we really want to go back to the old days, Bishop Mason was known for saying let the women alone, so they can do their work. Many of our churches were established by female church planters, including the church I pastor now. By biblical standards, these women would be apostles themselves.

Treating women as second-class citizens is as wrong and hateful as the days when we African Americans were treated as such. But what many women are saying to me is most of them do not want ordination. Those who do want ordination should be carefully considered and evaluated on an individual basis, just as I hope we do for men. And what about pastors' wives? Some wives are just partners in marriage, there to provide help and support, children, etc. But many pastors' wives are partners in ministry as well. They share the same calling as their husbands and they follow God's instructions too. If they are one in marriage, shouldn't they be one in ministry as well? The wives of our pastors should be treated as queens rather than burdens or non-entities for they are also responsible for our growth.

Questions continue with regard to female chaplains, and officially ordained women. We must come together to find a biblical solution that addresses the issue and honors God in all.

General Assembly

Many of us would be surprised at what is said on the floor of the General Assembly, or at Catfish Cabin. We say we have elected alcoholics, child molesters, adulterers, people with Mafia connections, homosexuals, etc. Why would we elect people with these kinds of reputations? If this is all speculation, we need to stop speaking so negatively. If true, though, we have a real problem. There isn't a single valid reason to elect that caliber of person as a leader. If we knowingly elect such people, then may God have mercy on us. An accountability process must be put in place to ensure to the best degree possible that leaders are worthy members of the Church of God in Christ. While we don't need to run down every rumor we hear, some of these rumors have been circulating for many years.

We've decided that God sees fit to keep each administration in place until death, with the exception of Bishop G.D. Owens. I have often wondered if that was God's doing or ours. In spite of the fact that we have elections every four years, we tend to reelect incumbents. If that continues to be the case, we should come up with a way to do that without the expensive ordeal, spiritually and financially, of an all-out election. Unless there is some gross misconduct, and sometimes even when there is misconduct, we reelect incumbents. As long as the General Assembly acts on a new process, I believe we meet the guidelines of our constitution. This way incumbents know their record will be reviewed, but we are spared the ordeal. Above all our arguments, agreements, and decision-making, though, God's wisdom and will should be at the core of our hearts.

Criteria for Pastors and Elders

When will we have unilateral criteria for pastors and elders? We need to stop spewing ignorance from the pulpit, and one way to accomplish this is to require certification for all pastors, old and new. We have the C.H. Mason System of Bible Schools, but we don't really use it or push it to the max, it is almost like an afterthought. Existing pastors can be grandfathered in, but all new pastors must meet the criteria. Those pastors who go to other seminaries should have our doctrinal training as well.

We get so much false and new age information through the media and other avenues, but where do we get the clear-cut doctrinal teaching of our church? It would be great to say in our conferences and conventions. Often, though, the preaching at these venues is a repetition of what we hear on television. Bishop G. E. Patterson was a great doctrinal preacher. Are there any left like him? While I thank God for Christian television and the ministry it provides, we don't need to get our teaching from it. Local and national assemblies and auxiliaries need to get their teaching from us.

Unfortunately, many of us in leadership don't seem to know Church of God in Christ doctrine.

Some preachers simply regurgitate sermons and ideas from others because they think it sounds good. We preach to get a reaction rather than a godly response - we want to leave everybody shouting. At this point I think God wants to say some things to us that will break our hearts and call us to repentance. We need an altar call for the saints. According to John G. Lake, one of the Azusa pioneers, a failure of the Azusa Revival was that "the people were more captured by the phenomena of God than by the person of God." In other words, we love what God is doing more than we love him. We are excited about the moves of God rather than with God himself. Consequently, our stand is constantly shifting from prophecy to worship to apostolic authority because we stand in what God is doing now rather than in who God is. We are tossed by every wind of doctrine instead of standing as a mature man in God.

Spiritual warfare is about standing and it takes the spiritually mature person to stand. Wrestlers come to the center of the ring and take a stance at the beginning of their matches. They push against one another to see if they ca n get the opponent to move or fall. They try to maneuver each other toward positions to maintain control. So, it is with us when we stand on the Word of God. The enemy has no control when it comes to God's Word because he is afraid of the word. That is why he has us doing so many unbiblical things in relation to him. Satan can control us when we do things other than as God's Word allows. He can do nothing with the Word itself except to try and choke it out of our lives,

King David's anointing was for him alone. It would not flow onto his brothers. It was the anointing that enabled him to encourage himself in the Lord when all was lost. The anointing brings release and recovery. Warfare is not a sign of being out of God's will or of defeat. It is a sign that we will recover it all.

Chapter 9

THE BLESSING OF HOMECOMING

Homecoming is a time of great joy and celebration. I remember as a child looking forward to the return of my older brothers and sisters for the holidays. It was always a time of rejoicing and familial unity. I look forward to this convocation like a great homecoming, and I'm sure we will celebrate as never before. Who is left among us who saw this house in its former glory and how do we see it now? God promised and it is so.

One of the things God has impressed upon my heart lately is that we need to go home by another way. After they had seen Jesus, the Wise men were instructed to return home another way. We need to return to the blessings and holiness of the previous generations, but we must do so by another way. We need to come home to prayer and praise but by another way. Becoming bogged down in the form and fashion of the past is a mistake. Rather than being caught up in a bunch of rules and regulations, we need to be caught up in our relationship with Jesus Christ.

Compared to some other denominations our church is young, but we are at least three or four generations deep as an aggregate movement. One of the problems with the third generation is that it does not possess the drive and vision of the first generation. The third generation usually only knows the stories of the past, but it has not experienced the God of its fathers. The latest generation of the Church of God in Christ is coasting on stories but is failing to learn from and become better because of past stories and examples. We can learn a few things from Abraham, Isaac, and Jacob. Abraham knew God for himself and it so impressed Isaac that Isaac wanted to know God for himself. Because Isaac lived a life committed to the Lord before his son, Jacob said to God when he left home, "God if you bring me back, if you let me come home, you will be my God, and I will bless you with my tithes and worship you forever." When God brought Jacob home some twenty years later, he committed. But God brought Jacob home another way. Though he left home as Jacob, a con man, trickster, and manipulator, he came back as Israel, one who is a prince and who prevails with God.

Homecoming is wonderful, but we can't come home the same way we left. We must let God change our name and nature. Adding to our faith for the purpose of productivity, we should be partakers of the Lord's divine nature.

Let us be like the Prodigal Son. He left home cocky and self-assured, rich in this world's goods, but life had some lessons to teach this young man before he would come back home. He lost all he had in riotous living, falling so low he was living and eating with pigs, an even more awful fate for a Jewish man. When life finished beating him up, the Prodigal Son got some sense, came to, and decided to go home. At least he would have food to eat and a place to sleep at home. And what a homecoming it was. His daddy was standing on the porch looking for him. Though he looked for his son's return every day, the father knew to allow his son to return to him. When it happened, he ran to him and kissed him and received him back as a son. Though he had left in finery, the son came home in rags, but the father called for the best robe and shoes of righteousness. A ring, the symbol of enduring and eternal love, was put on his finger.

Like the father in the parable, God is not coming after us, but he is waiting for our return. We want to come home but not to political games and foolery. We must come home to lives of service and leadership, to lives devoted to the glory of God. Choosing the best seats, congregational size competitions, and arguments over who is most righteous do not belong at a homecoming. Love and peace do.

We want to come home to Memphis, the place where it all got started. We want to come home to the headquarters of the Holy Spirit. We want to come home to the baptism of the Holy Spirit with the sign and seal of speaking in other tongues as the Spirit gives utterance. We want to come home to all night prayers and tarry meetings. We want to come home to the place where the saints danced and shouted till the walls would sweat. We want to come home to old time holiness and fire and brimstone preaching that scares Hell out of us and Heaven into us. We want to come home to a fellowship that is sweet as honey in the rock. We want to come home to the old landmarks. We want to come home where sons and daughters prophesy, where old men dream dreams and young men see visions. We want to come home to the prayer ministry and consecration of Bishop Mason. We want to come home to the anointed preaching and teaching that befits the Church of God in Christ, a family to which we belong and love. We want to come to the heart of God. We want to come home another way because in returning there is rest and restoration, healing and deliverance.

About the Author

Joseph T. Williams has served as Senior Pastor of Refuge Church of God in Christ for 38 years. After serving in a variety of ministry capacities under his father the Late Bishop D. Lawrence Williams, and his Brother Bishop David B. Williams during his tenure at Mason Memorial Church of God in Christ, the denomination's Mother Church in the State of Virginia, God elevated him to Pastor Refuge Mission in 1981. In his first service as Pastor, the small mission saw its membership more than double.

Pastor Williams has continued to lead that congregation through his exceptional preaching and teaching ministry. In addition to training pastors and church leaders he is a gift to the Body of Christ as a musician and psalmist with expertise in the ministry of Praise and Worship. And, he serves as Superintendent of the Chesapeake District, Church Historian, and leader of the Bible Institute for the Church of God in Christ, 2nd Jurisdiction of Virginia. He is founder and overseer of The Azusa Network (TAN), an apostolic family of churches, ministries, and leaders.

Pastor Williams holds a B.S. in Music Education from Nyack College in New York and a Master of Divinity with an emphasis in Christian Education from Virginia Union University School of Theology. He has been married to the love of his life, First Lady Brenda A. Williams, for more than 40 years. Their union has produced four children, all of whom faithfully serve the Church, and eight grandchildren.